ACCOUNTING
ETHICS
A PRACTICAL APPROACH

Howard J. Levine C.P.A.

Second Edition

© 2022 **Howard J. Levine**
ISBN: 978-1-7332595-5-2
Library of Congress Number: 2018904975

This book is dedicated to anybody who has ever faced an ethical situation and did not know what to do.

In other words, all of us.

TABLE OF CONTENTS

INTRODUCTION

"I had taken a course in Ethics. I read a thick textbook, heard the class discussions and came out of it saying I hadn't learned a thing I didn't know before about morals and what is right or wrong in human conduct."

—Carl Sandberg, American poet (1878–1967)

As you are about to discover, there are no right or wrong answers when discussing ethics. Each individual and business has their own ethical standards. Every society and religion has their own ethical beliefs. As hard as it may be to imagine, even governments and politicians have ethical requirements.

"Reputation is like fine china: Once broken it's very hard to repair."

—Abraham Lincoln, 16th president of the United States

In this book you will discover many of the fundamental ideas that shape our ethics. While ethics are not exclusively the dominion of the accounting profession, the public perception of accountants as independent, unbiased advisors requires that the highest ethical standards are understood, followed and maintained. There are specific laws and ethical standards that must be adhered to or unpleasant consequences may follow.

Note the emphasis on the practical, rather than just the theoretical, aspects of ethics. Many of the cases cited are from ethical lapses that became public because they were so large or large, well known or egregious. In this book you will find numerous "what would you do" cases taken from real-life situations involving a variety of individuals, businesses and organizations, all of which were encountered in a CPA practice. The names have been changed, but the questions remain. You get to determine, based on what you will learn and your own personal ethical standards, what you might advise or do in these situations.

This book is organized in two parts. The first three chapters discuss what ethics are, what influences your behavior and the concept of fraud:

Chapter 1—An overview of ethics. What influences our ethical makeup and the foundations of ethical decision-making?

Chapter 2—Foundations of ethical thinking. Various theories of what makes people ethical, plus why people and organizations cheat.

Chapter 3—Fraud. What exactly fraud is, and the elements needed for fraud and common fraud techniques.

The remainder of the book covers many laws, regulations and professional standards that CPAs are expected to adhere:

Chapter 4—Legal issues in ethics. Various federal laws and whistleblowing statutes.

Chapter 5—Accounting. AICPA Code of Professional Conduct, ethics for auditors and enforcement.

Chapter 6—Ethics for tax professionals. AICPA Tax Standards, IRS rules, tax fraud and penalties.

Chapter 7—California Accountancy Act. For those practicing or planning on doing accounting work in California, relationship to AICPA rules and specific statutes that apply to CPAs in California.

Chapter 8—Ethical leadership and how it applies to the accounting profession.

For consistency, throughout this book the term "CPA" refers to an accountant licensed by the applicable state(s) as well as those working in a CPA firm. It also may, depending on the jurisdiction, apply to non-CPAs and CPA candidates.

While the basic ethical principles don't change, rules, laws and regulations are frequently added, amended and modified. The citations in this book are accurate as of the publication date.

CPAs are used to a "right" answer, based on GAAP, FASB standards, laws or regulations; in many cases, making the ethical call is not that simple. In this book, the focus is for you to face these issues now, before they come up in practice, so you will be ready to act when the time comes. Unlike the quote at the start of this chapter, when you finish this book, you will understand ethics and be able to formulate your reactions to these difficult decisions.

CHAPTER 1

UNDERSTANDING ETHICS

"Do the right thing."

—Google's updated motto in its 2015 Code of Conduct,
replacing the original "Don't be evil" motto from 2004

Isn't it remarkable that a company that is so much a part of everyday life, who takes your personal data and sells it for profit, has this as their motto? Clearly Alphabet, Inc. (the corporate name for Google) believes this is ethical, but others may disagree. In this chapter you will explore the following:

- How ethics are defined
- What influences our personal ethics
- A guide to ethical decision- making

Ethics is commonly defined as "doing the right thing, based on individual, organizational or society standards." The term *ethics* comes from the Greek word *ethos*, meaning "custom." **Morals**, a term sometimes used when discussing why one acts, comes from the Latin word *mores*, meaning "manners and character."

While the words are frequently used interchangeably, they have very different meanings. Ethics are based on *external* sources, like codes of conduct for professionals, while *morals* are based on society and religious beliefs.

Just about every religion has their own definition of morals; Chart 1-1 summarizes many of these rules.

Chart 1-1

THE GOLDEN RULE IN THE WORLD RELIGIONS[1]

Judaism: What is hateful to you, do not do to your fellowman. This is the entire Law; all the rest is commentary. *Talmud, Shabbat 3id*

Christianity: All things whatsoever ye would that men should do to you, do ye so to them; for this is the law and the prophets. *Matthew 7:12*

Confucianism: Do not do to others what you would not like yourself. Then there will be no resentment against you, either in the family or in the state. *Analects 12:2*

Buddhism: Hurt not others in ways that you yourself would find hurtful. *Udana-Varga 5,1*

Hinduism: This is the sum of duty; do naught onto others what you would not have them do unto you. Mahabharata 5,1517

Islam: No one of you is a believer until he desires for his brother that which he desires for himself. *Sunnah*

Taoism: Regard your neighbor's gain as your gain, and your neighbor's loss as your own loss. *Tai Shang Kan Yin P'ien*

Zoroastrianism: That nature alone is good which refrains from doing another whatsoever is not good for itself. *Dadisten-I-dinik, 94,5*

Most of these rules basically state, in their own way, treat others like you want to be treated.

Frequently, taking the ethical path can be challenging, so another way to approach an ethical decision is to use what is called the "evening news" or "front page" approach, as illustrated in What Would You Do 1-1.

---

1. Retrieved from http://teachingvalues.com/goldenrule

WHAT WOULD YOU DO 1-1

Your six-year-old child attends a new school. On the first day of school, the teacher sends you a list of supplies necessary for the class (e.g., paper, pens, pencils). You work in a large corporation, so nobody would know if you take these supplies home for your kid.

What would you do?

Clearly this is a very small ("immaterial") amount, but it is, after all, stealing from your employer. Imagine how you would feel if you saw a video of yourself putting the supplies in your purse and walking out or a picture on the front page of the company newsletter as you placed the items in your backpack. Notice how ethical decisions are not always easy nor will everybody agree on what is ethical and what is not.

Concepts in Ethics

While ethics deal with how people or organizations should act, there are various aspects of everyday life that influence our actions.

Take the fact that being ethical is not the same thing as following the law. Benjamin Disraeli, the former prime minister of the United Kingdom, said "When men are pure, laws are useless; when men are corrupt, laws are broken."[2] In other words, ethical people don't need rules or laws since, based on their personal standards, they will strive to always do the right thing. On the other hand, having a law that prohibits certain actions will not stop unethical people (see, for example, Case 1-1).

Case 1-1

NORMAN HSU

Norman Hsu was a major Democratic Party fundraiser as well as the largest fundraiser for Hillary Clinton. In October 2008, he was charged by the Securities

---

2. Benjamin Disraeli, Edmund Gosse, and Robert Arnot. *The Works of Benjamin Disraeli, Earl of Beaconsfield, Embracing Novels, Romances, Plays, Poems, Biography, Short Stories and Great Speeches: Contarini Fleming, v. 2. Count Alarcos. Popanilla* New York and London, M. Walter Dunne,1904), Part 6, Chapter 3.

and Exchange Commission (SEC) with operating a $50 million Ponzi scheme in which he allegedly used investor funds to pay politicians and support his luxurious lifestyle. His companies promised investors, thru short-term financing to businesses, a return of 14% to 24% interest every 70 to 130 days.

Hsu did repay the investors interest and principal on time, so many of the investors either allowed the funds to roll over or made new investments. These investments were not legitimate, and Hsu defrauded at least 250 victims; plus, he was accused of violating election laws.

Hsu was convicted in 2009 to a term of twenty-four years for campaign finance violations and defrauding investors of over $20 million.[3]

Obviously, Hsu was not concerned with the law. But not everything is this clear-cut; sometimes the rules are not specific, resulting in a "gray area" (see What Would You Do 1-2).

WHAT WOULD YOU DO 1-2

Holding Payables

A nonprofit (exempt) organization keeps its books on the cash basis, recording expenses as they are paid rather than when the bills are incurred. At the end of the fiscal year, any unpaid bills are accrued so the financial statements can be prepared under **Generally Accepted Accounting Principles (GAAP)** and audited. This procedure is cost-effective for the organization and has consistently been done since the organization's inception over thirty years ago.

At a board meeting, interim financial statements are presented, showing that the organization is at a break-even point. A director is suspicious and looks into the executive director's drawer. She finds a stack of unpaid bills, the sum total of which are material to the organization's financial position and results of operations.

If you were the board member, how would you handle this situation? Does the discovery of the unrecorded payables have any effect on your perception of the organization? What about the ethics of the board member even looking into the drawer?

---

3. United States v. Hsu, 40 F. Supp. 2d 623 (E.D. Pa. 1999).

Clearly this organization is following their procedures by only reporting on the cash basis, but should the existence of the bills have been disclosed? Ethics are not set in stone but depend on the individual circumstances or even the organizational culture. Perhaps in this organization not reflecting the bills is the norm, but in another it would be an egregious violation of their rules.

Ethical lapses are even found on college campuses. Frequently, using a variety of methods, students cheat; some students believe their instructors cheat as well. A survey done by a company that performs private investigations and digital and business forensics found fascinating results (see Chart 1-2).

What can possibly justify this? In another study,[4] students rationalized their cheating in these ways:
— Denial of responsibility (e.g., too many hours at work, car broke down, family problems).
— Faculty and testing procedures (e.g., tricky exams that are unfair).
— Loyalty (e.g., more important to help a friend than avoid cheating).
— One student blamed society (i.e., "In America, we're taught that results aren't achieved through beneficial means but through the easiest means").

Cultural values will significantly influence ethics; different cultures and backgrounds affect how workers interact. Understanding cultural backgrounds are an important ingredient that will affect ethical behavior.

The single most important factor in building and sustaining an ethical business culture is the commitment of senior leadership. It influences employee perception and serves as a model of an organization's culture. Chart 1-3 reflects the perception of the "**tone at the top**" of senior executives' ethical behavior in various countries, from lowest to highest.[5]

---

4. Emily E. LaBeff, Robert E. Clark, Valerie J. Haines, and George M. Diekhoff, "Situational Ethics and College Student Cheating," *Sociological Inquiry* 60, no. 2 (May 1990): 190–97.
5. Alexandre Ardichvili, Douglas Jondle, and Brenda Kowske, "Dimensions of Ethical Business Cultures: Comparing Data from 13 Countries of Europe, Asia, and the Americas," *Human Resource Development International* 13, no. 3 (July 2010): 299–315.

Chart 1-2

COLLEGE CHEATING[6]

Kessler International queried 300 students who attend college in person and online. Some of the findings were as follows:

—Nine in ten (86%) admitted to cheating in some way in school.

—More than half (54%) thought cheating was OK, and some suggested that it was even necessary to stay competitive.

—Among those who acknowledged cheating, nearly all (97%) said they got away with it.

—Three-quarters of respondents (76%) said they had copied from somebody else's assignments.

—Slightly more (79%) admitted to plagiarism from internet sources.

—Nearly as many (72%) said they had used their mobile devices to cheat during class.

—A smaller number (42%) said they had purchased custom term papers or essays online.

—28% said they had a "service" take their online classes for them.

—Only 12% of students said they would never cheat because of ethics.

The survey also asked respondents about the ethics they believed their instructors had. Several said they knew of sexual exploits involving teachers and students that resulted in adjustments to grades, and others shared stories of faculty members taking bribes to change grades.

Some students feel that pressuring them to purchase books written by the faculty member in order to take the class is cheating by the instructor. In some instances, they said their instructors gave them test answers to ensure they passed their exams, particularly in cases where schools pressured faculty to pass their students.

Kessler observed that oftentimes unethical students turn into unethical job candidates. Based on their experience, they estimate as many as one in three job applicants lie about some aspect of their resumes, whether it's exaggerating their roles or claiming credentials never earned or positions never held.

---

6. Dian Schaffhauser, "9 in 10 Students Admit to Cheating in College, Suspect Faculty Do the Same," *Campus Technology, February 23, 2017, https://campustechnology.com/articles/2017/02/23/9-in-10-students-admit-to-cheating-in-college-suspect-faculty-do-the-same.aspx.*

Chart 1-3

TONE AT THE TOP

My company's senior management supports and practices high standards of ethical conduct.
>   **Low:** Japan, Italy
>   **Middle:** Netherlands, Germany, China, Mexico, Brazil, Saudi Arabia
>   **High:** Australia, United Kingdom, United States, India, Canada

My company strives to serve the interests of multiple stakeholders (e.g., customers, employees, suppliers, and community), not just the shareholders.
>   **Low:** Japan, Italy
>   **Middle:** Saudi Arabia, Mexico, China, Germany, Brazil, Netherlands, United Kingdom
>   **High:** Australia, United States, India, Canada

Where I work, people do not "get ahead" unless their behavior clearly demonstrates my company's values.
>   **Low:** Netherlands, Australia, Italy, Mexico, Brazil, Japan, United Kingdom, Canada, China, Germany
>   **Middle:** United States
>   **High:** India, Saudi Arabia

My organization has appropriate processes in place for me to report a policy violation.
>   **Low:** Japan, Italy
>   **Middle:** Netherlands, Mexico, Saudi Arabia, China, Germany
>   **High:** India, United Kingdom, United States, Canada, Australia

The results suggest that generally in the United Kingdom, United States, Canada, Australia and India, the top leadership of business organizations is perceived as playing a stronger role in promoting ethical cultures than in the rest of the nations surveyed.

The Six Pillars of Character

The Josephson Institute of Ethics has identified **Six Pillars of Character** that provide a foundation to ethical decision-making.[7] According to their research, following the letter of the law is not enough; we must also accept responsibility for our actions (or inactions). The six pillars are summarized as follows:

- Trustworthiness
- Respect
- Responsibility
- Fairness
- Caring
- Citizenship

Trustworthiness. Being trustworthy includes:

Honesty. We should tell the truth as we know it and without deception. This is the most basic of all ethical values, as discussed in What Would You Do 1-3.

WHAT WOULD YOU DO 1-3

Job Application

Maria recently graduated with a degree in accounting from a state university. She worked hard in school but could only achieve a 2.95 GPA, partially because she worked forty hours a week to pay her own way through college. Because the recruiters all had a minimum 3.0 GPA in her accounting major classes, Maria was unable to get an interview. In order to pay the bills, Maria stayed with her college job for another year but is anxious to start her public accounting career.

One day she reads about a job opening with a local CPA firm. The entry-level position pays little, but it's a way for Maria to get her foot in the door. She knows there will be candidates for the position with a higher GPA than hers, so she is thinking about using her overall GPA. When classes taken at the community college are factored in but not counted in the university computation, her GPA is 3.45. The advertisement asks for both GPAs.

Maria asks for your opinion before sending in the resume. What would you say to Maria and why? Is she being honest if she only includes one of the two GPAs on her resume?

7. Michael Josephson, *Making Ethical Decisions (Los Angeles: Josephson Institute of Ethics, 2002).*

Integrity. Integrity means acting on principle rather than what is easiest. Put simply, if you are told to do something wrong, you will not do it because it is just not right, as illustrated in What Would You Do 1-4.

What Would You Do 1-4
MEDICAL BILLING

Most physician offices are paid by insurance companies using a Current Procedural Terminology (CPT) code. CPT codes tell the insurance payer what procedures the healthcare provider would like to be reimbursed for. Within each code there are various levels of service; for example, a routine office visit might be Code 1, an extended visit may be Code 3 and a complex series of procedures might be Code 5.

You are the billing clerk for a surgeon and notice that the doctor codes just about every patient visit a "5," even the visits where the surgeon spends two minutes for a post-surgical check-up. You also notice that more and more insurance companies are requesting documentation for the patient visits. When you ask the doctor, she says not to worry about it and to stop questioning her judgment.

What should you do in this situation? Do you think that the physician is behaving with integrity? How about you?

Reliability. We make promises to others, and we have a moral, and sometimes also ethical, duty to follow up on these promises. This includes avoiding excuses and making commitments we have no intention of keeping. See how this might play out in What Would You Do 1-5.

WHAT WOULD YOU DO 1-5
World Series or the Opera

You agreed to go to an opera on Saturday night as part of your office group team building exercise. After work on Friday night, your friend calls and invites you to the World Series Game 7, which, of course, is the same night as the opera. You are no fan of opera and have never been to a World Series game.

What would you do? Would you suck it up and go to the opera or call your boss and say you suddenly became sick?

One additional thought on reliability: it affects your reputation. Once you get a reputation as somebody who is unreliable or a flake, it is difficult to shake. Keep in mind that Abe Lincoln quote mentioned earlier—"Reputation is like fine china: Once broken it's very hard to repair."

Loyalty. Loyalty means that others do not violate the confidence we place in them. For example, if you went to the World Series game in the What Would You Do 1-5 example, would you want your friend to tell your boss? Different cultures have different loyalty standards. In many cultures, loyalty to family and/ or the organization trumps all else, even criminal actions. Sometimes when you cover up something, it becomes public later, which can be even worse than the initial action.

Case 1-2

LARRY NASSAR[8]

Dr. Larry Nassar went to medical school at Michigan State University. In 1996, he became the chief medical coordinator for USA Gymnastics. He was also part of the faculty at Michigan State, where he taught and practiced medicine since 1997, meaning he wasn't only a renowned sports physician but also a faculty member of a public university.

In September 2015, Nassar abruptly retired from USA Gymnastics. A year later, a flood of sexual assault allegations began to explain why—more than 260 women accused him of sexual abuse, and in January 2018, he was sentenced to up to 175 years in prison in addition to sixty years for violating federal child pornography laws.

There is evidence that Michigan State University and USA Gymnastics, the two elite institutions associated with Nassar, were slow to act on reports that he was abusing girls and young women. On January 26, 2018, the entire board of USA Gymnastics agreed to resign. Hours after Nassar's sentencing on January 24, Michigan State president Lou Anna Simon announced she would step down. Michigan State's athletics director Mark Hollis announced his retirement on January 26.

---

8. Eric Levenson, "Larry Nassar Sentenced to up to 175 Years in Prison for Decades of Sexual Abuse," *Cable News, January 24, 2018, https://www.cnn.com/2018/01/24/us/larry-nassar-sentencing/index.html.*

Respect. Respect is treating others in a positive and dignified manner. To get respect, you must give it, which means respectful behavior should be part of how you act. Respect also assumes that, until proven otherwise, everybody deserves a basic amount of respect. And respect never goes out of style.

Case 1-3

RESPECT IN THE WORKPLACE[9]

Head Custodian Carl James worked for the Riverhead School District in New York for fifty-four years. Carl was the district's longest-serving employee and, at age seventy-nine, was the district's oldest living retiree, having begun his career as a school custodian. The school board president noted that Carl started when Dwight Eisenhower was president, four African American students began a sit-in at a segregated lunch counter in North Carolina, gas cost thirty-one cents a gallon, milk cost forty-nine cents a gallon and you could mail a letter for four cents.

Since Carl started there were many changes, but the board president said that the one thing that never changed was Carl's dedication, dependability and pride in his work.

In addition to giving Carl a plaque—which included a group photo of the February 1960 custodial staff—and proclamation, there was a special retirement gift from district officials: his chair, which, they joked, looked like it had been on the job as long as the head custodian. "We understand you've had this chair for 40 years," the school board president said, laughing, as the squeaky-wheeled, duct-taped desk chair was rolled over to Carl's seat in the audience. "We'd like you to keep it."

The school board could have just given Carl James his last paycheck and said "goodbye". Instead, they showed their appreciation for his service and, by having his family in attendance, their respect.

Responsibility. Responsibility is the willingness to accept accountability for your actions. Most jobs, whether you're waiting tables or managing large

---

9. Denise Civiletti, "Farewell and Thank You: Riverhead School Board Honors Retiring Staff," *RiverheadLOCAL, June 30, 2014, https://riverheadlocal.com/2014/06/30/farewell-and-thank-you-riverhead-school-board-honors-retiring-staff/.*

corporate accounts, require a certain amount of responsibility, as illustrated in What Would You Do 1-6.

WHAT WOULD YOU DO 1-6
Company Perks

Department and school chairs of most major universities are expected to attend conferences to present papers and network with their peers. These conferences are sponsored by other schools as well as by professional organizations.

A department chair of a public university attends a conference in another city for three nights. He is given a credit card he can use to charge the costs associated with the travel. As the accounts payable manager, it is your responsibility to review and approve all expenses over a certain amount. In reviewing the credit card bill, you notice that the department chair took a limousine to and from the airport, flew first class, stayed at a five-star hotel, ordered lobster for dinner and ran up a high hotel bar bill. The university policy is to pay for "reasonable" travel costs for conferences.

Do you believe the Chair's actions are ethical? How would you handle this situation?

Fairness. Fairness means treating others equally, impartially and openly. Josephson notes that "fairness implies adherence to a balanced standard of justice without relevance to one's own feelings or inclinations."[10]. What Would You Do 1-7 discusses "fairness" in a dilemma that teachers encounter.

---

10. Michael Josephson, *Making Ethical Decisions, (Los Angeles: Josephson Institute of Ethics, 2002), page 12.*

WHAT WOULD YOU DO 1-7

Teacher's Pet

You are teaching a college marketing class in which group work and participation are considered part of the grading scale. The syllabus states that the class is graded on a curve, with the highest group class average receiving an "A", second highest a "B" and all others a "C".

At the end of the term, Group #1 has a total score of 90.5 and Group #2 has a total score of 89.9. Group #1 pretty much never showed up in class and just turned in the work online, while Group #2 was in class every session, participating and adding to the cumulative knowledge of the course.

You can only give one "A" and one "B." How would you grade each group? Is that fair to the other group?

Note that the term "fairness" is even used in the standard auditor's report:

In our opinion, the financial statements referred to above, present fairly, in all material respects, the financial position of X Company as of [at] December 31, 20XX, and the results of its operations and its cash flows for the year then ended in conformity with accounting principles generally accepted in the United States of America.[11]

Caring. Caring is showing kindness and concern for others. **Empathy** is the ability to understand, be sensitive to, and care about others' feelings. Put another way, empathy is seeing from the other's perspective, as can be seen in What Would You Do 1-8.

---

11. AICPA Auditing Standards §508.08, *Reports on Financial Statements*

WHAT WOULD YOU DO 1-8

The Sick Co-Worker

You have an important project due this afternoon. As you walk into the office, you notice a key member of your team has red eyes and is coughing.

You could ignore their obvious discomfort. You could send them home to get well; if you did this, the project might not get completed on time. You could ask how they are doing, but if they say OK, would you really believe them and would they really be effective? What if you asked if they are all right and they told you about a personal tragedy in their life that you had no clue about?

Keeping in mind the project is due this afternoon, how would you handle this situation?

Citizenship. This doesn't mean voting or loving everything about the country you live or were born in but, rather, how we should behave as part of our community. This encompasses things like obeying the laws, voting and perhaps even volunteering.

Case 1-4

OXFAM AMERICA[12]

Oxfam America is a nonprofit organization whose domestic program was already active in the Gulf Coast states when the 2010 BP oil spill occurred. Building on its community links and backed by the shrewd use of national advocacy, the program was able to take advantage of the shock and turn it into opportunity. With that background in place, they helped ensure that compensation and other support was directly intended to benefit local people and communities—in particular by lobbying for legislation to get jobs for local people in the reconstruction effort. They had the community contacts in place to make it happen.

---

12. Duncan Green, "Advocating for Gulf Coast Restoration in the Wake of the Deepwater Horizon Oil Spill: The Oxfam America RESTORE Act Campaign," *Oxfam*, January 16, 2015, https://policy-practice.oxfam.org.uk/publications/advocating-for-gulf-coast-restoration-in-the-wake-of-the-deepwater-horizon-oil-338441.

As can be seen in What Would You Do 1-9, sometimes knowing who a good citizen is can be tricky.

WHAT WOULD YOU DO 1-9
Is My Client Really a Criminal?

One of your clients runs an organization that takes individuals with intellectual disabilities on trips and provides them with group events. The executive director is a single guy who really believes in the mission and helping others. Or so you thought, until you receive a phone call from him. He was arrested on twelve counts of child molestation charges. Despite his claims of innocence, he is convicted of a felony and sentenced to seven years in jail.

Now that you are aware of this, what factors should you consider when deciding if you should continue as the CPA for the organization?

The American Accounting Association suggests these seven steps when making an ethical decision:[13]

1. Determine the facts—who, what, where, when and how.
2. Identify the ethical issues.
3. Identify the norms by placing the decision in its social, ethical, and professional context. Also identify the major professional principles, rules and values.
4. Identify alternative courses of action by stating each one, without consideration of the norms, in order to ensure that each outcome is considered, however inappropriate it might be.
5. Assess the best course of action that is consistent with the norms, making it possible to see which options accord with the norms and which do not.
6. Consider consequences of the options.
7. Make a decision.

---

13. The American Accounting Association (AAA) Model, https://www.acowtancy.com/textbook/acca-p1/e1-ethical-theories/the-american-accounting-association-aaa-model/notes.

Ethics in the Accounting Profession

The objective of accounting is to provide relevant, timely information to help with decision making. CPAs must be trustworthy; otherwise users, such as lenders and investors, will not rely on their reports. It is not only CPAs who must be ethical. Managers and employees in private and governmental organizations must behave in an ethical manner when managing or running a business.

In term of ethics, CPAs score among the highest professions, placing seventh in the 2017 USA Today/Gallup poll of who Americans trust the most,[14] with CPAs ranking first among business professionals! The poll asked people to rank how they would rate the honesty and ethical standards, with nurses ranked as the most trusted.

CPAs received a 38% ("very high/high") and 51% ("average") for a net positive ranking of 81%. They scored very high compared to the rankings of lawyers (with a net of 26%), bankers (53%) and business executives (24%). Stockbrokers, at 7%, even beat Congress.

While this looks promising, as reflected in Chart 1-4, recent corporate scandals have not reflected on the accounting profession too well.

The largest professional body of CPAs is the **American Institute of Certified Public Accountants (AICPA).** This is a voluntary, membership association with CPAs in public, government, private and education fields. The AICPA also has student members. In addition to the AICPA, most states have CPA societies to serve their members.

Many accountants working in business are members of the **Institute of Management Accountants (IMA).** The IMA and AICPA both provide certification options and continuing education. They set professional standards for their members and emphasize that their members follow a code of ethics when performing their services. For internal auditors, there is an **Institute of Internal Auditors** with its own requirements and code of ethics.

Just about every country has its own accounting requirements and professional standards. In addition, the **International Federation of Accountants** is a global professional association.

---

14. Megan Brenan, "Nurses Keep Healthy Lead as Most Honest, Ethical Profession," *Gallup, December 26, 2017, http://news.gallup.com/poll/224639/nurses-keep-healthy-lead-honest-ethical-profession.aspx.*

Chart 1-4

RECENT ACCOUNTING SCANDALS

Company	Year	Nature of Scandal	Result
Waste Management, Inc.	1998	Over $1.7 billion of fake earnings	CEO & auditor found guilty. Shareholder suit settled for $457 million.
Enron	2001	Billions of dollars of debt kept off the balance sheet	CEO & auditor found guilty. Audit firm dissolved. Shareholder losses of $74 billion
Aurora Foods	2001	Understated expenses by $43.7 million to meet analysts' expectations	Corporate executives personally paid civil penalties
WorldCom	2002	Inflated assets by $11 billion	CEO & auditor found guilty. 30,000 job cuts & investor losses of $180 billion
Xerox	2002	Overreported $3 billion of equipment revenue	$10 million fine by SEC (largest ever)
HealthSouth	2003	Inflated earnings by $1.8 billion. Insider trading by billion	Senior executives found guilty
Bernie Madoff	2008	Ponzi scheme, defrauded 4,800 clients of $64.8 billion	Found guilty & ordered to pay $170 billion in restitution. Accountant also found guilty
Lehman Brothers	2008	Hid over $50 billion in loans	Company went bankrupt, 12,500 employees laid off

WHAT WOULD YOU DO 1-10
You Just Got Your License

You passed the Uniform CPA exam and received your license to practice accounting. You were fortunate enough to get a job with a large regional CPA firm and are excited to begin your new career.

In the first hour of orientation, the trainer asks who is a member of the AICPA; nobody raises their hand. He then asks who is a member of the state CPA society; again silence. The trainer goes on a rampage, saying how important it is to support your profession in any and all ways possible.

How would you respond to this?

Membership in these organizations is voluntary. In order to promote ethical standards in the public accounting profession, each state in the United States, plus four territories, has its own **Boards of Accountancy**. These boards not only license, but also regulate, licensed CPAs to ensure CPA's are following professional and regulatory standards. By doing so, these agencies protect the general public from unethical CPAs. There is also a **National Association of State Boards of Accountancy** that develops a uniform set of regulations states may adopt via the **Uniform Accountancy Act**.

As will be discussed in the next chapter, laws and regulations are not enough; as seen throughout this book, unethical people will ignore the law for their own gain.

Discussion Questions

1. What do you think it means to lead an ethical life?

2. Why do you think we need ethics in any profession, including accounting?

3. Based on this chapter and your own experiences, why do you think most people are uncomfortable discussing ethics?

4. Based on this chapter and your own ideas, why do your opinions and decisions on ethically charged issues matter?

5. Are there ethical differences between cheating on an exam, using somebody else's ID to get a drink at a bar and telling your girlfriend her hideous new haircut is flattering? Why do you feel this way?

6. Should employers use social media when considering interviewing you for a job? Should employers monitor your posts after you have been hired? Might you feel differently if you were the employer?

7. Using the Six Pillars of Character, discuss how each of the six steps are helpful to CPAs.

8. During your weekly study group, the topic of ethics comes up. The group discusses the role culture plays in ethics. Your childhood friend says that good ethics are universal and it does not matter where you come from, live or work. A foreign exchange student from another country disagrees, saying that things like paying bribes and cheating are common practices in their culture. Based on the concepts in this chapter, discuss the pros and cons of each argument and your opinion as to which is right.

9. You are graduating this semester and receive an offer from the accounting firm of Cut, Paste and Add, which you accept. Unexpectedly, you get an offer from another firm, Tick and Mark, which was really your first choice. They have given you one week to make the decision. What factors might you consider when pondering what to do next?

10. You are a project manager responsible for a decision that might lead to a huge opportunity for your company. If the company wins the bid, you will likely move into a senior management position; if you don't get the contract, it will probably be time to look for another job. To make matters worse, your employer is under financial pressure, so winning the contract could be a big positive turn of events while losing out to the competition might mean layoffs or even bankruptcy. Your contact at the client just emailed you a folder that appears to contain the bid of your main competitor!

   a. Would you look at the folder? Write a one-sentence answer for why you would or would not look.

   b. What is at stake here? How much should that matter to your decision?

   c.   Is there anything wrong with looking? Isn't business competition about doing your best to look out for your organization? Is it stealing or cheating? Why would you say that?

   d.   Does your answer about whether it is OK to look at the folder change if

      (1)   you knew your competitor would look at your folder if they were given the chance?

      (2)   you knew your boss supported you looking (or, alternatively, was strongly opposed to you doing so)?

      (3)   sharing bids is a fairly common practice in your industry?

Case Study[15]

In 2008, Virgin Mobile USA began a Strip2Clothe advertising campaign. Virgin Mobile's website said there were millions of homeless teenagers in the United States, and "someone out there needs clothes more than you." Virgin Mobile invited teenagers to upload videos of themselves taking off their clothes. For every uploaded striptease video, Virgin Mobile would donate a new piece of clothing, and for every five times the video was viewed, an additional piece of clothing would be donated. The strippers had to be eighteen or older, there could not be full nudity and Virgin Mobile would screen all the videos. Within a week there were twenty videos and 51,291 pieces of clothing were donated.

Needless to say, the campaign sparked immediate criticism. Parents were concerned that their underage children would strip, not tell their real age and post the video. One hundred and fifty charities objected to the campaign, saying that many homeless teenagers are sexually exploited and that the campaign contributed to the problem. Other arguments pointed out that the homeless normally need shelter and safety rather than clothes, plus the campaign was, simply put, in poor taste.

In response to this, Virgin Mobile altered its campaign. They launched a Blank2Clothe advertising campaign. Instead of stripping videos, they would post any talent video; for example, walking, juggling or singing. All of the striptease videos were taken down, and the strippers were asked to send in new, fully clothed videos.

---

15. Andrew LaVallee, "Virgin Mobile Pulls Back Racy Campaign," *Wall Street Journal, July 21, 2008, http://online.wsj.com/article/SB121660673649869421.html.*

Case Study Questions

1. Do you think that, despite the results, the criticism was justified? Why do you feel this way?

2. Do you believe that using marketing tactics that some might view as tasteless are also unethical? Why do you feel this way?

3. Provide examples of how this campaign might be viewed in different countries and cultures.

4. Name three criteria you can use to determine if advertising is ethical.

CHAPTER 2

FOUNDATIONS OF ETHICAL THINKING

"A man does what he must—in spite of personal consequences, in spite of obstacles and dangers and pressures—and that is the basis of all human morality."

—John F. Kennedy, 35th president of the United States

Moral philosophies help us decide what is right and wrong based on principles and rules. Before Adam Smith wrote his influential book outlining the basis of the free market,[1] he wrote a book on morals. That book, *The Theory of Moral Sentiments*, written in 1759, says that business should be guided by the morals of good people.[2] Even back then the concept of "tone at the top" was recognized as important. In this chapter you will be introduced to the following:

---

1. Adam Smith, *An Inquiry into the Nature and Causes of the Wealth of Nations* (London: W. Strahan and T. Cadwell, 1776)
2. Adam Smith, *The Theory of Moral Sentiments* (Edinburgh: A. Kincaid and J. Bell, 1759).

- Various theories as to what causes us to make ethical decisions
- A model that explains why people behave unethically, plus reasons why the model may not always be right
- How greed factors into ethical decision making

As with most philosophies, there are various theories. Some of the most common that apply to accounting and business decisions are discussed in the next section.

Teleology

The concept of **teleology** believes an act is morally right if it produces a desired result. Within teleology, **Egoism** believes consequences to the individual define acceptable behavior. Egoists believe they should make decisions to maximize their own self-interest; since we all have our own individual interests, one universal rule for all will not work. Finally, **ethical egoism** says each individual should always act morally, however they personally define it.

Egoism and *egotism* are quite different. For example, *egotists* often talk about themselves a lot. Egotists frequently do not listen to others, which is not good for making friends and generally makes people dislike them. In contrast, *egoists* frequently act humbly and pay attention to others because it is in their best interest to make people like them. *Egotism* is a character trait; *egoism* is a philosophy. Even so, you might think that egoists must secretly be egotists—and a lot of philosophers would agree with you.

If it sounds to you like egoism means "the ends justify the means," you're not alone. Many commentators believe egoistic people (and companies) are unethical and will not hesitate to take advantage of others to get what they want. We live in a capitalist society where the economic system encourages risk to make a profit. If you combine the theology theory with the profit motive, it is clear that, without some regulation, there will be problems.

Enlightened egoists take a long-range perspective that allows for the well-being of others. This helps them achieve an ultimate goal, but, of course, their own self-interest is still number one.[3]

---

3. O.C. Ferrell, John Fraedrich, and Linda Ferrell, *Business Ethics: Ethical Decision Making and Cases, 9th edition (Mason, OH: Cengage Learning, 2011), p.157.*

WHAT WOULD YOU DO 2-1

Missing the Deadline

Marco is in charge of the general ledger and financial statements of a large manufacturing company. There is a big presentation to a major lending institution on Friday morning. The financial statements must be completed and emailed to them by 5:00 Thursday night or the meeting will be cancelled and the company will have to start fresh with another institution.

As planned, Marco does the final review at 4:45 p.m. and something does not look right. A pit forms in his stomach as he notices that the provision for bad debts was never updated! Marco immediately calls the accounts receivable manager who is out for the day; there is nobody in that department who can help.

The vice president of finance has stressed that the company needs this infusion of cash, and the importance of the financial statements is critical to the meeting.

How would the concept of teleology guide Marco in this situation? What options should he consider?

Utilitarianism is a doctrine that says actions are right if they are useful or for the benefit of a majority. Simply put, they believe people should look beyond their own personal self-interest and impartially consider everybody affected, or potentially affected, by their actions. Their motto can be summarized as "the greatest good for the greatest number."[4]

Not all utilitarians agree on how this philosophy works. **Act utilitarians** believe that, if lying would produce the best consequences, they should lie.[5] In What Would You Do 2-1, using this philosophy, Marco might leave the financial statements as is so the company could obtain the funding.

---

4. Julia Driver, "The History of Utilitarianism," *Stanford Encyclopedia of Philosophy*, https://plato.stanford.edu/entries/utilitarianism-history/.
5. Manuel Velasques, Claire Andre, Thomas Shanks, S.J., and Michael J. Meyer, "Calculating Consequences: The Utilitarian Approach in Ethics," *Issues in Ethics* 2, no. 1 (Winter 1989).

Case 2-1

JOHN DELOREAN[6]

John DeLorean had a great career at General Motors and was ready to become the next president of GM. In 1973, he resigned and formed his own company. The DeLorean Motor Company made a two-seater sports car with gull wings. About nine thousand cars were manufactured in the next ten years, one of which was featured as the time machine in the *Back to the Future movies*.

While the cars were unique, the company continued to lose money. DeLorean was so committed to keeping the company afloat that he attempted to illegally sell cocaine to raise cash. When he was captured in a sting operation by the government, he admitted that he would do anything to delay and, hopefully avoid, the bankruptcy of his company.

Rule utilitarians believe that the best consequences happen when you follow the rules. Put another way, you select an action because it follows the moral rules everyone should follow. Using this philosophy in What Would You Do 2-1, Marco might speculate that the amount is likely immaterial and the financial statements can be issued as is. He might also insist on disclosure and, perhaps, bring an amended financial statement once the adjustment is determined.

Sidgwick's Dualism of Practical Reason is the middle ground between egoism and utilitarianism. Sidgwick argued that utilitarianism and egoism are in conflict and that neither theory is better justified than the other.[7]

Deontology

Deontology focuses on whether the action itself is right or wrong, as opposed to the consequences of those actions (**consequentialism**). To a deontologist, whether a situation is good or bad depends on whether the action that brought it about was right or wrong. What makes a choice "right" to a deontologist is its conformity with a moral norm.

---

6. Hillel Levin, *Grand Delusions: The Cosmic Career of John DeLorean (New York: Viking Press, 1983)*.
7. Alison Hills, "The Significance of the Dualism of Practical Reason," *Utilitas* 15, no. 3 (2003): 315–29, doi:10.1017/S0953820800004088.

Imagine that, in order to bring about a world without starvation, it was proposed to kill everyone who is not able to feed their family. A deontologist would argue that, because of the way in which it was brought about, a world without starvation would be wrong and they would oppose this action.[8]

Similar to utilitarians, deontologists are divided into those who those who apply rules to each unique circumstance (**act deontology**) and those who believe that basic moral principles guide their behavior (**rule deontology**). Act deontologists believe that actions are the proper basis on which to judge morality and to treat rules only as guidelines. Rule deontologists believe that there are some things we should never do.[9] For example, a rule deontologist would say it is wrong to steal clothing from a department store and give it to the homeless because it violates the store owner of their right to profit from the clothing. An act deontologist might feel that action is justified because it is the moral thing to do.

A favorite Latin proverb of deontologists is "Do what is right, though the world may perish." Consequentialists disagree; they would say that letting the world perish is the opposite of doing what's right. For deontologists, morality is not defined by consequences; a good action may have disastrous results, but that doesn't change the fact that it was the right thing to do. Consequentialists say that this is a dangerous philosophy because it allows people to justify horrible things, but deontologists reply that this is unlikely as long as the rules are true and just.[10]

Case 2-2

BEECH-NUT[11]

When the baby food maker was purchased by Nestle in 1979, CEO Neils Hoyvald promised the Nestle executives that Beech-Nut, which had been losing money, would become profitable in three years. Beech-Nut had a reputation for using high-quality ingredients in its baby food products; for example, its apple

---

8. Luke Mastin, "Deontology," *The Basics of Philosophy (January 2009), https://www.philosophybasics.com/branch_deontology.html.*

9. Ferrell, Fraedrich, and Ferrell, *Business Ethics (Boston, MA: Cengage Learning, 2017) p. 162*

10. Mastin, "Deontology."

11. United States of America v. Beech-Nut Nutrition Corporation, Niels L. Hoyvald, John F. Lavery, Zeev Kaplansky, Raymond H. Wells, Nina B. Williamson, South Orange Express, Inc., Danny Shaeffer (December 22, 1987) United States District Court, New York, 677 F. Supp 117 (E.D.N.Y. 1987), No. 86 CR 715

juice was advertised as 100% pure fruit juice, with no artificial flavoring, preservatives or coloring. The company and two of its executives, Hoyvald and John Lavery, who were responsible for manufacturing, were convicted of selling millions of bottles of apple juice for babies that they knew contained little or no apples.

At their trials, the two argued that they were being loyal corporate executives, making decisions that were necessary for the survival of the company, which was under intense financial and competitive pressures. They contended that their crime was, at worst, an error in judgment. While they were orchestrating a fraud against the consumers of the bogus apple juice (i.e., babies), they were model citizens with impeccable records. The attorney for Hoyvald described him as "a person we would be proud to have in our family."

Rights theories maintain that each of us has a worth or dignity that must be respected. This makes it wrong for others to abuse us or use us against our will. In other words, treating a person with dignity is allowing them the freedom to choose for himself.[12] A **right** is something morally good, justified or acceptable. A **duty** is a responsibility. In What Would You Do 2-1, the lender has the right to accurate financial statements while Marco has a duty to ensure that they are accurate.

The **social contract theory**, also known as *contractarianism*, says that people live together in society in accordance with an agreement that establishes moral and political rules of behavior. Proponents of this theory believe that if we live according to a social contract, we can live morally by our own choice and not because a divine being requires it.[13] As a member of society, each individual agrees to certain social norms. As a result, the values and norms developed by society must be fair to everyone who is a member of society.

Kantian ethics is based on the work of Immanuel Kant, who thought that placing the emphasis on happiness completely misunderstood human nature. In his view, the basis for our sense of what is good or bad, right or wrong, is our awareness that human beings are free, rational agents who should be given appropriate respect.[14] This concept can be seen in What Would You Do 2-2.

---

12. Velasques, "Calculating Consequences".
13. McCombs School of Business, "Social Contract Theory," *Ethics Unwrapped, accessed June 3, 2018, http://ethicsunwrapped.utexas.edu/glossary/social-contract-theory.*
14. Emrys Westacott, "Kantian Ethics in a Nutshell: The Moral Philosophy of Immanuel Kant," *ThoughtCo.*, January 2018, https://www.thoughtco.com/kantian-ethics-moral-philosophy-immanuel-kant-4045398.

WHAT WOULD YOU DO 2-2

Who Is More Respected?

You pick up the newspaper and read about a local businessman who donated $20 million to the local hospital for a new cancer wing. You see a photo of him and his wife handing over the check as their names are hoisted to the top of the building. They are surrounded by admiring friends, politicians and family.

On your way home, as you are stopped at a traffic light, you observe a gardener handing a homeless person $5 and an apple.

Which of these two people do you respect more? Why?

The Becker Rational Model

When people act dishonestly to obtain an undeserved benefit, they are cheating. A ballplayer may "cheat" with a little more pine tar on the bat. In cards you may "cheat" by sneaking a peek at another's hand. And in business one may "cheat" by padding an expense report. Note that cheating may or may not be acceptable based on the various ethical models discussed so far.

Nobel Prize winner Gary Becker looks at cheating as no different from any other financial decision—if the benefits exceed the costs, people will cheat. In other words, it is basically a cost accounting problem in which one compares the marginal benefits against the marginal costs.[15] This is called the **Becker Rational Model** (see Chart 2-1).

Chart 2-1

BECKER RATIONAL MODEL

People cheat according to the following formula:

When the Expected Value of Benefits > (Expected Probability of Detection) x (Expected Magnitude of Punishment).

---

15. Gary S. Becker, "Crime and Punishment: An Economic Approach," *Journal of Political Economy* 76, no. 2 (March–April 1968): 169–217.

On the surface this seems very logical. Not a lot of people would look at their friend's exam when sitting in the front row of the classroom with the professor right in front of them. Nor would you steal a candy bar when the clerk is staring at you. But there are quite a few flaws in this simple model. This chapter will review a few of them:

- Impulsive behavior
- Dead presidents effect
- No Detection Model
- No Punishment Model

Impulsive behavior can influence cheating. The Becker Rational Model assumes people perform mental calculations, either literally or subconsciously, before cheating. In reality, many people act without calculating the odds of being discovered or what the severity of punishment may be.

Case 2-3

JOHN RIGAS

John Rigas was the founder and CEO of publicly traded Adelphia Communications. At seventy-seven years old, he was a billionaire who owned several houses and a professional hockey team. He committed accounting fraud that cheated the company and investors.

While he may have believed that the Expected Probability of Detection was small, the Expected Magnitude of Punishment was huge (he was sentenced to fifteen years while his son, the CFO, was sentenced to twenty years).[16] It is hard to imagine that the Expected Value of Benefits exceeded the value of spending the rest of his life in prison.

The **Dead presidents effect** recognizes how physical money, as compared with other items of value, has a lot of emotional impact (dead presidents are on paper money, thus the name). According to the Becker Rational Model, the Expected Value of Benefits is the same, no matter if it is cash or other property.

---

16. Thomas S. Mulligan and Water Hamilton, "John Rigas Is Sentenced to 15 Years," *Los Angeles Times*, June 21, 2015, *http://articles.latimes.com/2005/jun/21/business/fi-rigas21.*

In reality, people are much more likely to cheat when benefits are in the form of property rather than money. What Would You Do 2-3 presents various options to illustrate the impact of this theory.

WHAT WOULD YOU DO 2-3
Dead Presidents

Given these options, which is more likely for you to try and get away with:
Take a ream of paper from the office or steal $5 from petty cash?
Falsify a $1,000 company check or improperly add a week's vacation to your accrual?
Ask the company for a cash loan or manipulate an issue date of a stock option?

The Becker Rational Model predicts that people would be cheaters if they face little risk of detection. Real life gets in the way when other factors, such as morals or ethics, come into play. The **no detection model** recognizes that some people who have virtually no chance of detection still won't cheat.

Case 2-4

CHANCE OF DETECTION

Researchers ran an experiment where people were randomly assigned into two groups. In Group "A" the subjects were asked to do a few short tasks, count up the tasks completed and collect their winnings from an unmonitored cash drawer. Group "B" did the exact same tasks, but their scores and cash withdrawals were carefully monitored. Not unexpectedly, Group "A" claimed more winnings than Group "B". Also, Group "B" reported their scores much more meticulously, only claiming the prize money that they deserved.[17]

This brings up the question when dealing with a real-life example in What Would You Do 2-4.

17. Nina Mazar, On Amir, and Dan Ariely, "The Dishonesty of Honest People: A Theory of Self-Concept Maintenance," *Journal of Marketing Research* 45, no. 6 (December 2008): 633–44.

> ## WHAT WOULD YOU DO 2-4
>
> ### Inventory Question
>
> Jane owns a furniture store with three locations. It is the end of the fiscal year and profits are not where they should be; in fact, it looks like there will be a loss. Jane has some significant debt and, without a profit, it is likely the line of credit will not be renewed.
>
> You are the CPA and notice that some of the inventory counts look a bit funny; the stores could not possibly own that many couches! When you ask Jane about it, she smiles and says, "We have count sheets, which I have approved, so don't stress over it. Even if they are a bit high, the documentation is there so we are covered."
>
> How do you feel about this? What would you do in this situation?

The **no punishment model** recognizes that some people will not cheat even when there is no possibility of punishment.

Case 2-5

PANERA BREAD

In 2010, Panera Bread decided to conduct a social experiment. They opened a store in an affluent neighborhood of Chicago that ran on a pay-what-you-want model. The business model was to essentially shame the affluent members of the neighborhood into subsidizing meals for those who were poor. Customers could pay the $5.89 "suggested" price, more, less or nothing. The experiment initially worked; Panera Bread discovered that the patrons did not exploit the opportunity to save money by paying less and essentially cheating the company.

As an aside, after a few months and the initial advertising was over, customers stopped realizing the option to pay whatever they want existed, and the average payment became only 75% of the suggested price. This cost the company a significant amount of money and that was the end of the Panera Bread social experiment.[18]

---

18. Lydia DePillis, "Panera's Pay-as-you-go Pricing Experiment Failed. Here's How They Could Fix It," *Washington Post*, July 14, 2013, https://www.washingtonpost.com/news/wonk/wp/2013/07/14/down-with-price-tags-heres-how-to-profit-when-people-pay-what-they-want/?utm_term=.4d6dfc34e6a4.

Keeping in mind the social experiment of Panera Bread, What Would You Do 2-5 looks at the no punishment model from another angle.

WHAT WOULD YOU DO 2-5

Missing Lotto Tickets

Juan works at a convenience store where, among other things, they sell state scratch-off state lotto tickets. As the outside CPA, Juan confides to you that it would be really easy to steal lotto tickets, since, especially during the graveyard shift, there is only one employee and the security cameras can easily be blocked. Of course, you are apprehensive since this is a poor internal control. Upon further investigation, whenever Juan is working, there has never been a shortage. Other employees, yes, but not Juan.

How would you discuss this situation with the owner of the store? Do you believe that most employees are as honest as Juan?

Cheating

Clearly there are many models as to why people are dishonest. Cheaters may believe it is all right to cheat because of one or more of the following:

- Rationalization
- Priming
- Loss aversion effect
- Depleted resistance
- Copycat effect
- Cheater's high

Case 2-6

CHEATING AND SELF-ESTEEM

Two groups of participants took an IQ test and waited to learn their results in a room with a large mirror. Researchers arbitrarily told everybody in one group that they had done poorly and told another group that their results were impressive. The participants in the group that performed miserably left the room rapidly, apparently disgusted and unable to look themselves in the mirror. Those that performed well stayed far longer and admired their images in the mirror.[19]

In business, cheating might provide economic rewards, but it can also generate remorse, which then threatens the cheaters' positive view of themselves. You can relate this to the Becker Rational Model by looking at it as a management accounting formula; people will only cheat up to the level at which the incremental rewards from cheating are greater than the incremental harm done to their self-perception. Thus, people who care about complying with social norms and have a good self-image rarely cheat. Alternatively, those who place a low importance on their view of themselves often will cheat extensively. What Would You Do 2-7 gives an example of an easy incentive to cheat.

WHAT WOULD YOU DO 2-6

An Unexpected Discount

Basketball season is coming up and you go to the local sporting goods store to purchase some new shoes. You find the right size and bring them to the cashier. The cashier is distracted, and instead of charging you $50, he only rings up $5, so the total he asks for is $5.41, including tax.
      What would you do?

Many cheaters will use **rationalization** to explain their cheating. This can be accomplished in many ways. Some people will rationalize their behavior by saying that they deserve the benefits derived from cheating. This allows them to increase their cheating while minimizing harm to their self-image, as can be seen in What Would You Do 2-7.

---

19. Shelley Duval and Robert Wicklund, *A Theory of Objective Self-Awareness (Oxford, England: Academic Press, 1972).*

WHAT WOULD YOU DO 2-7

A Great Job

You have just finished an income tax return for a large client. In preparing the return, you noticed they overpaid sales tax on some purchases and were able to file for a huge refund. That plus the efficiency of your work resulted in less billable hours than budgeted.

Promotions are around the corner and a significant component of your evaluation will be the billable hours over the past year. Other than yourself, if you added some hours, nobody would ever know.

What would you do? And how do you rationalize your choice?

Another way to rationalize cheating is to argue the cheating is minor. An example of this is a client who files a false tax return with the justification that the government is so big and wastes the money. Or the salesman who adds some miles to his reimbursement request because "the company can afford it."

Many people will rationalize their stealing if it has a low cost to their employer. Recall What Would You Do 1-1, where you considered taking work supplies home for your child's schooling. If you had taken the supplies, you might have rationalized your actions by arguing that they are immaterial, the employer makes a lot of money anyway or everybody does it so you can too.

A final rationalization is cheating when the facts are uncertain or ambiguous, as in What Would You Do 2-8.

WHAT WOULD YOU DO 2-8

Applying for a Bank Loan

You are purchasing a car and the bank asked you to complete the necessary paperwork. One of the questions asks if you are involved in any current or pending litigation.

Unfortunately, last week you were involved in an auto accident where you rear-ended another car and clearly were at fault. While you have auto insurance, the other party is claiming significant damage to their car, plus whiplash and other injuries that, if proven, might exceed your insurance coverage. At this point, the attorneys for the other party are talking with your insurance carrier.

Do you disclose the accident on the loan application?

Known as **priming**, people who are reminded of religious principles moments before they are about to cheat are more likely to behave ethically than those who are not.

Case 2-7

FRUSTRATED PROFESSOR

Professor Thomas Tang of Middle Tennessee State University was frustrated. The cheating in his MBA class that, of all things, had just covered a section on ethics, had gotten out of hand, so he tried an unusual approach. Each student was asked to sign an exam pledge that stated, as punishment for cheating, "I will be sorry for the rest of my life and go to Hell." As expected, some students called the department chair and complained that they were asked to sign this, which they found offensive.

Tang said he based his pledge on an academic study showing students who read the Ten Commandments before an exam were less likely to cheat, but he would probably leave that statement out in the future.[20]

One would expect that people who possess strong religious commitments would behave more ethically than others at work. Based on studies, the evidence is inconclusive.[21]

Of course, nonreligious moral reminders work as well. For example, when one must sign a document under penalty of perjury, you would expect that most people would think twice about the consequences of not telling the truth.

Some people are so afraid of the negative side of a transaction that they will make more of an effort (and even incur costs) to avoid a loss than they will to obtain a gain. This is known as **the loss aversion effect.**

---

20. Marc Abrahams, "Hell-raising prof inspired by Ig Nobel winner," *Improbable Research,* *November 5, 2009, https://www.improbable.com/2009/11/05/hell-raising-prof-inspired-by-ig-nobel-winner/.*
21. Nigel Barber, "The Human Beast: Are Religious People More Ethical in Their Conduct?", *Psychology Today, May 7, 2009, https://www.psychologytoday.com/us/blog/the-human-beast/200904/ethical-conduct-in-the-moral-right.*

Case 2-8

WINNER OR LOSER?

People were asked to choose between two results. If they choose the first option, they would definitely lose $750. The second option was an outcome that gave a 75% chance of losing $1,000 and a 25% chance of no loss. Statistically both of these choices had an average expected loss of $750. The study showed that nearly nine out of ten chose the second one, hoping to avoid losing anything.[22]

In business, this loss aversion shows up in many ethical decisions. For example, people who have an expected refund from the IRS cheat at a fairly low rate because they anticipate the pleasurable gain of receiving a tax refund. Contrast this to the fact that taxpayers who unexpectedly look like they will owe taxes are far more likely to cheat to avoid the loss of having to pay the additional taxes to the government.[23]

We all know somebody with a lack of willpower. Perhaps they compulsively spend, have an unhealthy diet or don't exercise. Anybody who is on a diet knows that willpower goes down when you are overworked. Similarly, studies have confirmed that being tired and anxious makes us more likely to stray from our ethical values.[24] This is called **depleted resistance** and has a significant effect on our decisions.

Case 2-9

MAKING GOOD DECISIONS

In an experiment on cheating, the participants were put into two groups. Group 1 consisted of people whose energy levels peak late in the day (night owls) while Group 2 were people whose body rhythms were a bit more consistent throughout

22. Daniel Kahneman and Amos Tversky, "Prospect Theory: An Analysis of Decision under Risk," *Econmetrica 47, no. 2 (March 1979): 263–91.*

23. Peter J. Reilly, "Study Shows Taxpayers with Balance Due More Likely to Cheat," *Forbes Magazine, October 17, 2013, https://www.forbes.com/sites/peterjreilly/2013/10/17/study-shows-taxpayers-with-balance-due-more-likely-to-cheat/#2241e73f35f9.*

24. Roy F. Baumeister and John Tierney, *Willpower: Rediscovering the Greatest Human Strength (London: Penguin Books, 2011), 2–3.*

the day (morning people). Each of the groups played a game at various times of the day and reposted their scores, with higher scored earning better prizes.

The night owls were much more likely to cheat in the early morning hours when their energy levels were low. Not surprisingly, morning people cheated more frequently towards the end of the day when fatigue set in.[25]

The results are clear—employees should be sure to make ethically sensitive decisions when their willpower is not depleted!

The **copycat effect** is also a justification for cheating. If you have been to a ball game or concert and watched a couple sneak into better seats, and then another does the same, you have experienced this firsthand. What Would You Do 2-9 is another example of this effect.

WHAT WOULD YOU DO 2-9

Cheating on an Exam

You are taking an exam online with internet access. As soon as the professor turns her head, the person sitting next to you opens a new web browser and looks up the question. The student on the other side does the same and the person in front of you is doing so as well. In fact, just about every student whose screen you can see has two browsers open.

Would you do the same? Would your answer change if the exam was graded on a curve?

In the workplace, a good manager will either terminate or transfer an unethical employee before the others are contaminated with that unethical conduct.

Some people love to get away with cheating and actually get what is called a **cheater's high**, which is the pleasure of getting away with it. This can be in just about any business setting where somebody has stolen funds or inventory. Frequently they will gloat and occasionally even brag to maintain the euphoria even longer.

---

25. Brian C. Gunia, Christopher M. Barnes, and Sunita Sah, "The Morality of Larks and Owls: Unethical Behavior Depends on Chronotype and Time of Day," *Psychological Science* 25, no. 12 (October 6, 2014): 2272–74.

This is not just a human phenomenon; even animals cheat! According to anthropologists, the frequency of what we refer to as cheating is directly correlated with the size of the specie's outer brain layer (the neocortex). Humans have the biggest neocortex.[26]

Cheating will never be eradicated, but companies are trying to reduce it by enforcing strict codes of conduct and encouraging whistleblowers to speak up. Many CPA firms do background checks on prospective employees, including occasionally hiring outside firms to verify that the potential employee has integrity. They also monitor social media for clues as to unethical conduct. Many employers also engage in loss prevention by purchasing a fidelity bond.

Greed

Simply put, **greed** is not just wanting to be rich but, rather, striving for more wealth than a person reasonably needs. According to an old proverb, gluttony and greed are reached when a person's "eye is larger than his belly." Greed is not necessarily a good thing; as Leonardo da Vinci once said, "He who wishes to be rich within a day will be hanged within a year."

Greed is also considered one of the seven deadly sins. According to theology, the punishment in Hell for greed is to be boiled alive in oil. Of course, it would be the finest, most luxurious boiling oil money can buy, but it's still boiling.[27]

The quest for material wealth elevates the chemical dopamine in our brains, making us feel good. In fact, many people prefer the "chase" for great wealth and are sort of let down at the "catch". Greedy people are not necessarily unethical or cheaters (although, in some cases, they are); they just want more, as illustrated in What Would You Do 2-10.

26. Hans Kummer, *Primate Societies: Group Techniques of Ecological Adaptation (Chicago: Aldine Transaction, 1971).*
27. Adam Shannon, "The Sin of Greed," *Seven Deadly Sins, accessed June 3, 2018, http://www. deadlysins.com/greed/.*

WHAT WOULD YOU DO 2-10

Blackjack

Blackjack is a card game of chance where you are betting to get the highest card against the dealer. In many casinos, the odds are basically break even (the house advantage is as small as .02%). Compare that to other games found in a casino, where the house odds can be as high as 33%.[28]

You are in Las Vegas for a friend's bachelor party and are playing blackjack. You brought $500 with which to gamble. So far, luck has been with you and your $500 has almost doubled; you are looking at $950 of chips. This is your last night and are leaving the next day.

What might motivate you to continue and try to increase your winnings? What might cause you to stop and be happy with what you have? Would the fact that your mortgage is due next month and you are a little short influence your decision?

Discussion Questions

1. Using the three concepts of teleology, what drives a free market system?

2. Choose an event in your life where you believe you acted ethically. Discuss the event in terms of the teleological frameworks discussed in the text.

3. Using the same event you chose in question 2, discuss the event in terms of the deontological frameworks.

4. Do you believe our moralities trigger our actions, or do we act and then justify our actions by changing our moralities? Explain your answer.

5. Describe some of the moral and social factors that go into ethical decision-making.

6. Describe an experience in your workplace when you were ethically challenged. If you have not had such an experience, choose a personal example. How did you resolve the dilemma?

---

28. Michael Shackleford, "House Edge of Casino Games Compared," *The Wizard of Odds*, December 9, 2013, https://wizardofodds.com/gambling/house-edge/.

7. Describe and explain an example of a business decision that would be unethical even though it is legal.

8. What would an Act utilitarian and a Rule utilitarian say differently when evaluating the same case?

9. What is the major contrast between Utilitarianism and Kantian ethics?

10. Using the example from this chapter, discuss whether you should follow your self-interest or your moral principles.

11. You are the executive director of a religious organization and are responsible for all purchasing decisions. The organization has a need for some printing. Your husband is a printer, and you award the job to him.

    a. Which of the concepts of Deontology would be appropriate when making this decision?
    b. Assume you were questioned by a member of the board of directors. How might you rationalize this decision?
    c. Do you think this is an ethical decision? Why?

12. You have been looking for a house for the past nine months and found the one you really want. As part of the home loan application, the bank asks to see your most recent Forms W-2 and tax returns. Your income level barely qualifies for the loan; should rates go up even a fraction, you probably will not get the loan or the house. You can make the payments but don't want to blow the deal.

    You have always done your own taxes and are considering printing (but not mailing to the IRS) another tax return to show some additional income.

    a. Your friend just got a loan with the same bank. She tells you that this bank does not verify this data with any outside parties. Should you submit the fake tax returns? Why?
    b. Relate the concepts of cheating discussed in this chapter to how you would make this decision.

13. You attend a charity silent auction and, surprisingly, win the bid for a trip to Africa. You bid $2,500 and the value of the trip is over $5,000, so you are extremely excited. When the mail arrives, you get another surprise; when the charity sent a donation letter they just acknowledged the $2,500 as a charitable contribution, even though that amount is clearly not deductible. It's time to do your taxes.

    a. Relate the concepts of cheating discussed in this chapter to how you would decide to deduct the $2,500.
    b. Do you think it is greedy to take the deduction? Why?
    c. Would you do it?

14. Among other things, your organization supports in-home day care providers by reimbursing them for food given to preschool children. This government-sponsored program has given thousands of meals to poor children throughout the area.

    In order to be sure that the providers are legitimate, your organization has monitors who visit the homes at least once a quarter. This internal control seems to be working well until you make a surprising discovery—one of the recipients does not exist! It seems that one of your monitors made up a provider's name and address, including direct deposit information, and took the money herself to the tune of $70,000. When you confront her about this, she is unrepentant, saying the providers get plenty of government assistance and are taking advantage of the system and she can do more good with it than they are doing.

    a. How do the concepts of teleology and egoism allow this person to justify her actions?
    b. Do you believe she is right? Does this fit into your personal morals?

Case Study

Sometimes an entrepreneur will do anything to keep the business alive, even to the point of breaking the law.

Chris Neary was successful in the advertising industry. He had worked as the marketing director for TELUS Communications, a wireless telephone company, and in 2007, at age thirty-one, he started his own advertising agency, just before the 2008 recession. He was forced to refinance his home twice in order to keep his business going. As he came close to bankruptcy, Chris decided to smuggle about 50 kilograms of marijuana from Canada into Seattle and earn about $10,000, equal to one month's cash flow.

On April 26, 2010, he and four others were arrested in Washington State and charged with drug-trafficking. On September 27, 2010, Chris was sentenced to eight months in prison for conspiracy to import marijuana, with two years of probation that could be served in Canada.

Why would Chris even try such a plan? In a published interview, Chris admitted that he was desperate to save his business. "I was so hell-bent on making my business the same kind of success I've had in the rest of my career, I just overlooked the ramifications of it," he said. He continued, "I felt it was up to me to turn things around and I tried to do everything myself. I didn't ask anyone's opinion on it. I just did it." Chris acknowledged how dumb this was and cooperated fully with the authorities. He admitted his mistake and how this event changed his life. "I've had humility slap me in the face, and I want to stay accountable to it and move forward."[29]

Case Study Questions

1. Why do you think a business owner would become so committed to his business he would intentionally engage in an illegal activity?

2. What ethical principles did Chris ignore? Which principles might have justified his actions?

3. Assume that after he serves his eight-month sentence, Chris starts another advertising agency with a new partner. Do you believe that Chris has any ethical responsibility to reveal his drug-trafficking conviction to his new partner before they started the business? Why do you feel this way?

---

29. Brennan Clarke, "Potential Payoff for Gruelling Trek Turns into Drug Charges," *The Globe and Mail*, June 9, 2010, https://www.theglobeandmail.com/news/british-columbia/potential-payoff-for-gruelling-trek-turns-into-drug-charges/article4389575/.

CHAPTER 3

FRAUD

"Rather fail by honor than succeed by fraud."

—*Sophocles, Ancient Greek playwright and philosopher (497–406 BCE)*

Fraud is generally defined as wrongful or criminal deception intended to result in financial or personal gain. The courts are filled with cases of fraud; this chapter will discuss the basic concepts of fraud and how they relate to accounting. In this chapter you will explore the following:

- The effect of fraud on companies
- The fraud triangle
- Common fraud techniques

The most recent Annual Global Fraud Survey, commissioned by Kroll and carried out by the Economist Intelligence Unit, polled 768 senior executives worldwide from a broad range of industries. Some of the findings are shown in Chart 3-1.

Chart 3-1[1]

COMPANIES AFFECTED BY AND VULNERABLE TO FRAUD

TYPE OF FRAUD	PERCENTAGE OF COMPANIES AFFECTED IN PAST 12 MONTHS	PERCENTAGE OF COMPANIES DESCRIBING THEMSELVES AS HIGHLY OR MODERATELY VULNERABLE
Information theft	29%	56%
Theft of physical assets	27%	57%
Management conflict of interest	26%	52%
Internal financial fraud	23%	52%
Corruption and bribery	21%	50%
Vendor, supplier or procurement fraud	20%	51%
Regulatory or compliance breach	20%	49%
Misappropriation of company funds	20%	48%
Money laundering	16%	43%
Market collusion	19%	50%

As can be seen in Chart 3-1, 29% of the executives said that the information theft was the most common fraud experienced. Theft of physical assets (27%) and management conflict of interest (26%) were the next two most frequent types of fraud they experienced. Information theft is up from 24% in the 2016 survey.

But these incidents only tell part of the story; the incidence of fraud continued to climb. Overall, 84% of surveyed executives report their company fell victim to at least one instance of fraud in the past 12 months, up from 82% in 2016. This represents a continuous, year-on-year rise since 2012, when the reported incidence was 61%.

Contrary to the common perception that the United States is a low-fraud place to do business, it is a country with a fraud problem just like any other; the US companies surveyed show figures very close to the global average. The overall prevalence (91% of companies affected by at least one fraud in the past year) was 7% above

1. Kroll, *Global Fraud Report: Vulnerabilities on the Rise,* https://www.kroll.com/en/insights/publications/global-fraud-and-risk-report-2018.

the global average. For the top 5 frauds shown in Chart 3-1, in every case the United States had a significantly higher incidence of fraud than the global average.

The survey also shows that the United States has a substantial problem with insider fraud; when a fraud occurred in the past year and the perpetrator was known, 30% of the American respondents said that a senior or middle manager had been a major player in at least one such crime. Junior employees were reported by nearly half (48%) of the companies as being the main perpetrator of fraud that their organization had experienced.

The Association of Certified Fraud Examiners (ACFE) does an annual study of occupational fraud. Some of the results of the most recent study can be found in Chart 3-2.

Chart 3-2[2]

OCCUPATIONAL FRAUD

—The typical organization loses 5% of revenue in a given year as a result of fraud.

—The total losses to the organizations in the study exceeded $6.3 billion, with an average loss per company of $2.7 million.

—The median loss for all companies in the study was $150,000, with 23.2% of the companies having losses of $1 million or more.

—Asset misappropriation was by far the most common form of occupational fraud, occurring in more than 83% of those reported but causing the smallest median loss of $125,000. Financial statement fraud was on the other end of the spectrum, occurring in less than 10% of the organizations but causing a median loss of $975,000. Corruption cases fell in the middle, hitting 35.4% of the companies with a median loss of $200,000.

—Among the various forms of asset misappropriation, billing and check tampering schemes posed the greatest risk based on their relative frequency and median loss.

—The longer a fraud lasted, the greater the financial damage it caused. The median duration of the frauds was eighteen months, but the losses rose as the duration increased. Those schemes that lasted more than five years caused a median loss of $850,000.

---

2. Association of Certified Fraud Examiners, *Report to the Nations on Occupational Fraud and Abuse: 2016 Global Fraud Study*, accessed May 29, 2018, http://www.acfe.com/rttn2016.aspx.

—In 94.5% of the organizations, the perpetrator took some efforts to conceal the fraud. The most common concealment methods were creating and altering physical documents.

—The most common detection method was tips (39.1% of cases). Organizations that had reporting hotlines were much more likely to detect fraud through tips than organizations without hotlines (47.3% and 28.2%, respectively).

—When fraud was uncovered through active detection methods, such as surveillance and monitoring or account reconciliation, the median loss and median duration of the schemes were lower than when the schemes were detected through passive methods, such as notification by police or by accidental discovery.

—In cases detected by either an outsider or insider tip at organizations with formal fraud reporting mechanisms, telephone hotlines were the most commonly used method (39.5%). However, tips submitted via email (34.1%) and web-based or online forms (23.5%) combined to make reporting more common through the internet than by telephone.

—About two-thirds of the organizations hit by fraud were privately held or publicly owned companies. These for-profit organizations suffered the largest median losses among the types of organizations analyzed, at $180,000 and $178,000, respectively.

—Of the cases involving a government victim, those that occurred at the federal level reported the highest median loss ($194,000), compared to state or provincial ($100,000) and local entities ($80,000).

—Surprisingly, the median loss suffered by small organizations (those with fewer than 100 employees) was the same as that incurred by the largest organizations (those with more than 10,000 employees). Even so, this type of loss is likely to have a much greater impact on smaller organizations.

—Among the various forms of asset misappropriation, billing and check tampering schemes posed the greatest risk based on their relative frequency and median loss.

—Organizations of different sizes seem to have different fraud risks. Corruption was more prevalent in larger organizations, while check tampering, skimming, payroll, and cash larceny schemes were twice as common in small organizations as in larger organizations

—The banking and financial services, government and public admin-istration, and manufacturing industries were the likely sectors for fraud.

—Although mining and wholesale trade had the fewest cases of any industry, those industries reported the greatest median losses of $500,000 and $450,000, respectively.

—Consistent with previous studies, external audits of the finan-cial statements were the most commonly implemented anti-fraud control. Nearly 82% of the organizations underwent independent audits, and 81.1% of organizations had a code of conduct in place at the time the fraud occurred. Note how this did not find or prevent these frauds.

—Small organizations had a significantly lower implementation rate of anti-fraud controls than large organizations.

—The presence of anti-fraud controls was correlated with both lower fraud losses and quicker detection.

—The most prominent organizational weakness was poor internal controls, which was cited in 29.3% of cases, followed by an override of existing internal controls, which contributed to just over 20% of cases.

—The perpetrator's level of authority was strongly correlated with the size of the fraud. The median loss in a scheme committed by an owner/executive was $703,000. This was over four times higher than the median loss caused by managers ($173,000) and nearly 11 times higher than the loss caused by employees ($65,000).

—More occupational frauds originated in the accounting department (16.6%) than in any other business unit. More than three-quarters of the frauds were committed by individuals working in seven key departments: accounting, operations, sales, executive/upper man-agement, customer service, purchasing, and finance.

—The more individuals involved in an occupational fraud scheme, the higher losses tended to be. The median loss caused by a single per-petrator was $85,000. When two people conspired, the median loss was $150,000; three conspirators caused $220,000 in losses; four caused $294,000; and for schemes with five or more perpetrators, the median loss was $633,000.

—Fraud perpetrators tended to display behavioral warning signs when they were engaged in their crimes. The most common red flags were living beyond their means, financial difficulties, unusually close association with a vendor or customer, excessive control issues, a general "wheeler-dealer" attitude combined with unscrupulous behavior. Many were recently experiencing family problems, such as a recent divorce. At least one of these red flags was exhibited during the fraud in 78.9% of cases.

—In 40.7% of the companies, the victim organizations decided not to refer their fraud cases to law enforcement, with fear of bad publicity being the most-cited reason.

—Of those prosecuted, 23.1% resulted in a civil suit, and 80.8% of completed suits led to either a judgment for the victim or a settlement.

The Fraud Triangle

Most businesses and auditors assess the threat of fraud using what is called the **Fraud Triangle**. Like its name implies, the fraud triangle has three elements: Incentives and Pressures, Opportunity and Rationalization (see Chart 3-3).

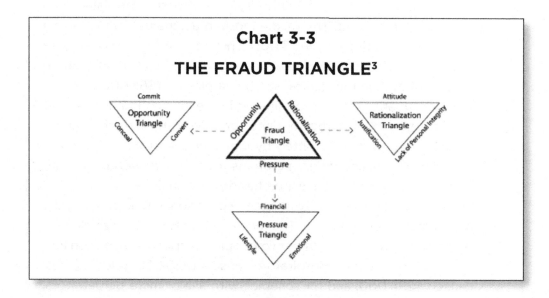

Chart 3-3

THE FRAUD TRIANGLE[3]

---

3. Marshall B. Romney, "Fraud," *Grolier Online, accessed May 27, 2018, http://go.grolier.com/ print?id=0111790–0&type=0ta&product_id=gme&authcode=gme.*

Opportunity is the way an individual will defraud the organization. For a fraud to occur, there must be an unexpected good chance or a favorable circumstance. Sometimes even a temporary situation may arise where there is an opportunity to commit a fraud without a high chance of being caught. Unless a company is actively working to prevent fraud, repeated opportunities for fraud may occur.

Case 3-1

LOCKE AND JENKINS[4]

The SEC filed a complaint against Locke Capital Management, Inc. and Leila C. Jenkins, its founder and sole owner, in March 2009, alleging that they invented a billion-dollar client in order to gain credibility and attract legitimate investors. The Complaint further alleged that Jenkins tried to perpetuate her scheme by lying to the Commission staff about the existence of the invented client and furnishing the Commission's staff with bogus documents in 2008, including fake custodial statements that she created on her laptop.

The US District Court ordered that Locke and Jenkins were jointly and severally liable for disgorgement of $1,781,520, representing advisory fees paid to them from 2007–2009, plus prejudgment interest of $110,956. In addition, each defendant was ordered to pay a penalty of $1,781,520. In February 2012, in separate administrative proceedings filed by the Commission against Jenkins and Locke, an administrative law judge barred them from associating with any broker, dealer or investment adviser and from acting as an investment adviser.

When preventing fraud, opportunity is the most important factor to consider. If you eliminate opportunities for fraud to be committed, it can be greatly reduced. Because there is little chance that losses will be recovered once the fraud has already occurred, preventing fraud is also much cheaper for companies than detecting it later. What Would You Do 3-1 illustrates when an opportunity to steal is available.

---

4. US Securities and Exchange Commission, Litigation Release No. 22349, *Securities and Exchange Commission v. Locke Capital Management, Inc. and Leila C. Jenkins*, Civil Action No. 09-CV-100-WES (D.R.I.), April 30, 2012.

WHAT WOULD YOU DO 3-1

Stealing from Your Brother

You are the owner of a small heating and air conditioning contracting company, with annual revenues of about $750,000 and five employees. One of your employees is your sister, who also serves as the bookkeeper, responsible for cash receipts and paying vendors. Neither you nor your sister is highly computer literate, so all of the books are maintained by hand.

Business has been steady, with new construction and repairs keeping your crew busy every day, but you notice profits do not seem to be what you expect. Your sister says she is on top of it, collecting all of the receivables, and perhaps the company rates are too low.

Your sister is out one day and you make a bank deposit. In looking at the deposit slip, you notice the amount you put in the bank is not the amount reflected in the books; in fact, the books are higher than what went into the bank. You call your outside CPA who discovers that the cash receipts journals do not add up to what the bank says; all of the cash receipts are listed, but the column adds to another amount. In every case, the deposit is off by one or two checks.

You call the bank and are informed that those checks were deposited into your sister's personal account. Apparently, this has been going on for five years and totals over $100,000.

In retrospect, how could you have prevented this opportunity to steal? And now that you know it was done, how could you prevent it in the future? Also, do you sue your sister and/or file a police report?

Opportunity is where internal controls come into play. The more internal controls a company has designed and implemented, the less opportunity there should be for employees to commit fraud. It is important that the internal controls are effective and efficient or the benefit will be greatly reduced. Internal controls may include segregation of duties, supervision, and information technology controls (passwords, hand scanners, etc.).

Rationalization is how the individual manages to justify what he or she is about to do or has done. Some may think they are just going to "borrow" the stolen goods or that they need the money more than the "big" company they are stealing from. Frequently, individuals claim they are not paid what they are worth.

Case 3-2

TYCO[5]

Tyco's former CEO Dennis Koslowski, former CFO, Mark Swartz, and former general counsel, Mark Belnick, were accused of giving themselves interest-free or very low interest loans (sometimes disguised as bonuses) that were never approved by the Tyco board or repaid. They were also accused of selling their company stock without telling investors as required under SEC rules.

Koslowski, Swartz, and Belnick stole $600 million from Tyco International through their unapproved bonuses, loans, and extravagant "company" spending. A $6,000 gold-plated shower curtain, a $2,000 trash can, and a $2 million birthday party for Koslowski's wife in Italy are just a few examples of the misuse of company funds. As many as 40 Tyco executives took loans that were later "forgiven" as part of Tyco's loan-forgiveness program, although it was said many did not know they were doing anything wrong. Hush money was also paid to those the company feared would "rat out" Kozlowski.

Essentially, they concealed their illegal actions by keeping them out of the accounting books and away from the eyes of shareholders and board members. The rationalization used by the perpetrators could have been that they worked hard for the company and therefore deserved the extra compensation. Also, they may have thought they would eventually pay it back. Overall though, the main motivation in the scandal was greed.

One way to prevent fraud is to keep individuals from ever being able to rationalize the behavior in the first place. Companies can create a zero tolerance policy towards fraudulent behavior, plus remind employees and customers of this policy on a regular basis. Companies can also make certain that individuals know the cost of fraud to other customers and other employees. Letting individuals know there are heavy consequences makes it more difficult to minimize unethical behavior. What Would You Do 3-2 presents how rationalization is used.

---

5. Securities and Exchange Commission v. L. Dennis Kozlowski, Mark H. Swartz and Mark A. Belnick, United States District Court, Southern District of New York, September 11, 2002.

WHAT WOULD YOU DO 3-2

All You Can Eat Buffet

You are at the local Sizzler getting the "all you can eat buffet." Your friend is not too hungry and just orders a hamburger, but, after seeing the delicious desserts asks you to get her a piece of cake. Dessert does not come with a hamburger but is available to those who pay for the buffet.

How might you rationalize getting something from the buffet that you did not pay for? Would you do it? Why?

The final part of the Fraud Triangle is **pressure**. Most individuals require some form of incentive or pressure to commit a criminal act. This pressure does not necessarily need to make sense to outside observers, but it does need to be present. Pressures can include money problems, gambling debts, alcohol or drug addiction, and overwhelming medical bills. Greed can also become a pressure, but it usually needs to be associated with injustice; for example, "The boss does it, why can't I?"

Case 3-3

WELLS FARGO BANK[6]

In 2016, Wells Fargo Bank was fined $100 million for widespread unlawful sales practices. The Bank's employees secretly opened accounts and shifted funds from consumers' existing accounts into these new accounts without their knowledge or permission to do so, often racking up fees or other charges.

The bank had compensation programs for its employees that encouraged them to sign up existing clients for deposit accounts, credit cards, debit cards, and online banking. According to the enforcement action, thousands of Wells Fargo employees illegally enrolled consumers in these products and services without the customer's knowledge or consent in order to obtain a bonus for meeting sales targets. They did it by transferring funds from consumers' existing accounts to the new account, for which the employee got credit and a bonus.

---

6. Jeff Ehrlich, *Hundreds of thousands of accounts secretly created by Wells Fargo Bank employees leads to historic $100 million fine from the CFPB, U. S. Consumer Financial Protection Bureau, September 8, 2016.*

These illegal sales practices dated back at least five years. They included using consumer names and personal information to create hundreds of thousands of unauthorized deposit and credit card accounts.

Companies only have so much impact on the personal lives of customers and employees. Identifying any possible pressures, such as money problems and substance abuse, can be helpful. Working to relieve these issues can help prevent criminal behavior. What Would You Do 3-3 illustrates a case where personal motivations can cause an effect on behavior.

WHAT WOULD YOU DO 3-3

End of the Fiscal Year

You are the executive director of a nonprofit organization. It is the end of the December 31st fiscal year, and your revenues are $25,000 short of your budgeted target. The organization has a matching grant with the federal government and, unless this target is met, the federal funds may be in jeopardy, as will your bonus and, potentially, your job.

During the second week of January, over $30,000 of checks come in. The checks are all dated in January.

How do you handle this situation? Do you record the donations so you can meet the target even though they came after the year end?

As can be seen with these examples, the Fraud Triangle has many components; generally, all of them must be in place for a successful fraud to take place. Case 3-4 shows how it all fits together in one case.

Case 3-4

SOUTH CAROLINA HOSPITALITY ASSOCIATION[7]

In 2012, Rachel Duncan was sentenced to thirty months in federal prison and ordered to repay $367,508 in restitution to the Hospitality Association of South Carolina (HASC). Ms. Duncan had been the accountant for the HASC. She

---

7. Kelly Wessel, "Case Studies: The Fraud Triangle and the South Carolina Hospitality Association," *Wessel Accounting, March 27, 2013, from https://www.wesselaccounting.com.*

was hired in 2001 after HASC's previous bookkeeper was fired for embezzling money.

Opportunity. Nothing is known about the embezzlement committed by the bookkeeper previous to Ms. Duncan, other than after she was dismissed, internal controls were reviewed and strengthened to prevent future losses. Ms. Duncan became acclimated to her new responsibilities and procedures and proved to be a competent and trustworthy employee. As her tenure lengthened, she was given more responsibility and oversight of her responsibilities was decreased. Procedures established after the previous embezzlement were relaxed as confidence in Ms. Duncan's abilities increased and as a friendship between her and the CEO developed. She eventually became responsible for nine bank accounts and began to write and sign checks, including payroll checks, and make deposits.

Pressure. Investigators discovered that Ms. Duncan had a gambling addiction that started with video poker then escalated to online gambling when South Carolina outlawed video poker in 1999. The stolen funds were diverted into Ms. Duncan's personal bank account; from there, money was wired to offshore gambling payment processors.

Rationalization. Ms. Duncan used the funds she stole to feed her addiction and didn't appear to be motivated by anything else. She was contrite in her confession and sentencing, most likely justifying her actions by believing future gambling winnings would allow her to repay all of the stolen funds.

Common Fraud Techniques

It is important to note that misstatements on financial statements may not necessarily be fraud, but, rather, an error. This can be as simple as poor management judgment on an accounting estimate or not knowing about an outstanding invoice. Many errors are immaterial to the organization and not necessarily fraud. What Would You Do 3-4 presents a common dilemma.

WHAT WOULD YOU DO 3-4

The Absentee Accountant

You are the controller of a vitamin manufacturer with about $10 million of sales and a net income of $2 million. Sales are made to wholesalers throughout the country. Your accounting team consists of three other employees who, respectively, handle accounts receivable/sales, accounts payable/inventory and payroll.

The accounts payable/inventory clerk has been out for a medical procedure and the other two employees had to pick up the slack. At the December 31st end of the fiscal year, everything looked good, and the books were closed. On February 28th, the auditors presented a report that contained a clean opinion.

On March 10th, almost two and a half months after the year-end, a shipment of vitamins was returned. The vitamins, which were shipped on December 15th of the previous year, were found to be moldy. Because this is a major customer, the president insisted that the $100,000 purchase price be refunded.

Do you restate the financial statements? What are the ramifications of your decision, both if you do restate and if you decide not to? If bonuses are involved, would that change your opinion?

People who commit fraud are usually intent on achieving their goal. Looking at past fraud cases and how the fraudster thought they might get away with it can provide valuable insight for CPAs. Some of the ways to commit fraud include the following:

- Manipulating revenues
- Round-trip transactions
- Altering expense estimates
- Improper capitalization of expenses
- Manipulating allocations
- Hiding liabilities and debts
- Ponzi schemes
- Tax cheating

Over 60% of companies guilty of accounting fraud inflated their income. Some of the most common techniques to **manipulate revenues** are as follows:

- Create fictitious customers and/or phony sales invoices
- **Channel stuffing**, that is, selling more merchandise to customers than they need by rewarding them for their cooperation
- Recording a sale even though it is likely that a significant portion will be returned
- Recording sales prior to the goods being shipped
- Recording revenues on long-term contracts prior to them actually being earned
- Exaggerating the market value of appreciating assets
- Recording sales to poor credit customers, knowing that many of the accounts receivable will not be collectible.

Case 3-5

PARMALAT[8]

Parmalat is an Italian dairy producer. When Parmalat's financial performance began to slip in 1990, rather than resolve its problems, management chose to hide them through fraud and collusion. During the next thirteen years, Parmalat executives used a wide range of unethical techniques to extend the fraud. They inflated revenues by creating fake transactions and double billing. They used receivables from these fake sales as collateral to borrow more money from banks. They created fake assets that inflated reported assets. They took on debt that they hid from the bank. They also worked with investment bankers to move debt off the balance sheet and disguised some of it as equity on the balance sheet.

There is evidence they colluded with the auditors. For example, Parmalat's books showed they sold huge quantities of powdered milk to Cuba. Had the auditors compared these sales quantities to the total size of the Cuban market, it would have been obvious something was going on. The fraud was eventually uncovered; investors lost $20 billion.

---

8. Ron Rimkus, CFA, "Parmalat," *Financial Scandals, Scoundrels & Crises*, November 26, 2016, https://www.econcrises.org/2016/11/29/parmalat/ .

A **round-trip transaction** is a prearranged plan where a company sells an asset to inflate its revenue and agrees to buy back essentially the same asset. This is typically done around the end of an accounting period.

Case 3-6

KRISPY KREME[9]

Krispy Kreme is a publicly traded corporation, but many of the stores are franchised. In each of three separate quarters during fiscal 2004, Krispy Kreme engaged in round-trip transactions related to the reacquisition of a franchise. In all three of the transactions, Krispy Kreme paid money to the franchisee, and the following quarter, the franchisee paid the money back to Krispy Kreme as prearranged. On the payback, Krispy Kreme recorded additional income about equal to the funds originally paid during the prior quarter to the franchisee.

An example of one of these transactions was when Krispy Kreme reacquired a franchise in Texas; Krispy Kreme artificially increased the price it paid for the franchise. In return for this, the franchisee agreed to purchase, from Krispy Kreme, specific doughnut-making equipment. When the deal closed, Krispy Kreme paid the additional amount to the franchisee (capitalizing this as an acquisition cost) and then debited the franchisee's bank account for the equipment (showing this as revenue). This technique boosted Krispy Kreme's after-tax net income for the quarter by approximately $365,000, even though there was no cash effect.

A **side agreement** is a secret deal parties form to hide their main agreement. For example, a company makes a sale of $1,000 and verbally allows the buyer to take a 20% credit in sixty days when they pay. The sale is recorded at $1,000 when, in reality, all the seller expects to collect is $800.

---

9. Securities and Exchange Commission, Release No. 59499, Administrative Proceeding File No. 3-13388, In the Matter of Krispy Kreme Doughnuts, Inc., March 4, 2009.

Case 3-7

TYSON[10]

An Arkansas chicken company needed a bigger freezer. As is common in this sort of deal, they entered into a contract with a builder to sell the land on which the freezer would be built and then lease it back for six years; they retained an option to buy the property and freezer at the end of the lease at the fair-market value. A side agreement actually changed the price of buying the property to the difference between the lease payments and the construction costs plus interest. In other words, the chicken company pretended to have a lease, but it actually had a loan because of the side agreement. Since it was concerned with violating usury laws, the company did not tell its lawyer, accountants, bank and, because the main agreement allowed the company to pay lower taxes (they could deduct the lease payments), the IRS.

Tyson subsequently bought the chicken company, and Tyson was not told about the agreement until after the purchase. The builder took out a loan and used the freezer as collateral, not mentioning the side agreement to Tyson or its own bank. Later, when they discovered the side agreement, Tyson wanted to exercise its option to buy the freezer at the side agreement price; the builder would actually owe money to Tyson since interest rates had decreased so much!

As an aside, Tyson was unable to enforce the side agreement. A court ruled that this sort of side agreement is unenforceable against the government, who had taken over the bankrupt bank.

The **matching principle** of accounting matches revenues with associated costs. While on the revenue side of the equation there are always some estimates necessary, there are many more estimates necessary to properly record expenses. For example, estimating an allowance for bad debts, contingent liabilities and warranty exposure all are based on judgment and can be manipulated to achieve a desired result. As can be seen in What Would You Do 3-5, **altering expense estimates** is a common manipulative, and sometimes fraudulent, accounting technique.

10. Mary Wood, "Side Agreements Have Important Implications for Contract Law, Theory, Cohen Says," University of Virginia School of Law, November 16, 2006, https://content.law.virginia.edu/news/200611/side-agreements-have-important-implications-contract-law-theory-cohen-says.

WHAT WOULD YOU DO 3-5

How Long Does a Building Last?

You are the CPA for a nonprofit organization that has rehabilitated a 200-year-old building into a museum. The cost of about $20 million was paid by a grant to the organization, and you now have a $20 million asset on the books.

In discussions with the building contractor, they say that, while the basic structural components will last longer, in about twenty years much of the work will be obsolete. Based on this, you determine to depreciate the improvements over a twenty-year life. You run this by the auditor, who agrees that this is reasonable.

Over the history of the organization, they have generally broken even; revenues cover the expenses. The director of development, who raises money, is concerned that the non-cash charge of $1 million depreciation expense every year will make the organization show a deficit each year for the next twenty years, which will greatly complicate her fundraising efforts. Since it is a 200-year-old building, and depreciation is a non-cash charge, she is pushing for a seventy-five-year life.

How would you react to this? Would the fact that this organization does not pay taxes factor into your decision? What about if they did?

Most accounting fraud is for underreporting expenses, but sometimes overreporting can be fraudulent as well. In **cookie jar accounting**, an organization will deliberately overstate their expenses in the current year—when they are more profitable—and reverse the expenses to a more reasonable amount in future years, when they need a higher net income. In some cases, this is perfectly legal (e.g., a salesman, having already met his quota, waits to close a sale until the next quarter), but other times it can be manipulative. What Would You Do 3-6 illustrates a common scenario.

WHAT WOULD YOU DO 3-6
Annual Bonus

You are the vice president of marketing of a regional bank. If the net income of the bank exceeds $10 million, you get a bonus. This year the bank is doing well, comfortably above the $10 million net income. There is talk of a recession in the next few months, and you are concerned the bank will not meet this target next year.

One of the major estimates a bank must make is its provision for loan losses; in other words, what loans will not be repaid and how much of a reserve should be set up for it. This is, of course, a judgment call based on a number of factors.

Under the cover of "conservatism," would it be appropriate to push up the allowance a bit in the current year so next year you will have a better opportunity to get that bonus? What factors would you consider in making this decision?

In many of the large accounting fraud cases there was **improper capitalization of expenses**. For example, if the company knows auditors only look at fixed asset additions over $10,000, they might capitalize anything below that, no matter what the asset is, thus increasing reported net income.

Case 3-8

WORLDCOM[11]

Before it filed for bankruptcy, WorldCom was the second largest international telecommunications company in the United States. Their margins were small so they came up with a very simple way to boost profits.

When a customer places a phone call overseas, most phone companies generally have to use other companies' phone lines. For example, if you made a call from the United States to Japan, WorldCom would pay the Japanese phone company for completing the call (i.e., connecting to their line). While these are clearly

---

11. Dennis R. Beresford, Nicholas deB. Katzenbach, C.B. Rogers, Jr., *Report of Investigation by The Special Investigative Committee of The Board of Directors of Worldcom, Inc., March 31, 2003, https://www.sec.gov/Archives/edgar/data/723527/000093176303001862/dex991.htm.*

period costs (expenses), WorldCom improperly capitalized billions of dollars as "Line Costs," amortizing them over a period of time. This is sort of like paying your monthly cell phone bill and debiting it as an asset.

The amazing part of this fraud is not that they did it but that they got away with it for so long. Eventually the internal auditors discovered what was going on and reported it to the audit committee, who then reported it to the SEC for enforcement action.

In many transactions there can be **allocation estimates**. For example, you purchase a building; how much of the cost goes to the land (not depreciated), improvements (depreciated over a short period of time) and the building itself (depreciated over a longer period of time)? If you sell a computer program, how much of the revenue is for the software (amortized over the estimated useful life) and how much for the phone support (expensed if less than one year)? As illustrated in What Would You Do 3-7, by manipulating allocations one can easily affect the outcome of financial statements.

WHAT WOULD YOU DO 3-7
Reporting Grant Expenditures

Many social service nonprofit organizations have various sources of revenues—including federal, state and local grants, fundraising events, individual donations and corporate gifts. Most of the government grants require some form of reporting.

As the CPA for a social service organization, you are asked to come up with a way to report the expenses for each grant. In looking at the services provided you see that, essentially, you are "making money" on the government grants, which then subsidize some of the other programs, including the administrative and fundraising operations. You know that the organization will be audited by the governmental agencies but also want to help ensure that the organization can keep on providing the needed community services.

What factors should you consider in making the allocation model? How does the fact that you want to have the organization financially viable influence your decision?

Hiding debts by not recording the liability is a common way of improperly manipulating the financial statements. Sometimes these are called **off-balance sheet liabilities** and have resulted in many large frauds. Chart 3-4 shows an example of how this works.

Chart 3-4

HIDING LIABILITIES

Here is an example of one way a company would hide its liabilities.

1. Just before the end of a quarter, a company purportedly sells a poorly performing loan and uses this cash to repay debt. The journal entry would be:

Cash	100	
Asset		100
Note Payable	100	
Cash		100

No problem at this point—the company has removed questionable assets and reduced its debts. Investors and auditors like that.

2. Shortly after the end of the quarter, the company reverses the above transaction by repurchasing the asset and re-establishing the liability. Combined, the two entries balance each other out, but the company has effectively made its balance sheet look artificially improved with just the touch of a few keys.

Note that this is specifically not acceptable under Accounting Standards Update 2014-10.

In a **Ponzi scheme,** a devious promoter entices gullible investors by promising profits that are too good to be true. After raising funding, the promoter makes good on his promise by paying the initial investors the promised return on a timely basis. These investors think they have hit upon something amazing and tell their friends, relatives and fellow workers, who also make investments. Eventually, the swindler disappears with the money.

How does the promoter get such returns? They never do. The promoter basically pays the promised return with money raised from others, not earnings. He generally accompanies the payments with false financial statements showing big profits, at least until he can no longer be found (see Case 3-9).

Case 3-9

BERNIE MADOFF

Bernie Madoff almost got away with the largest Ponzi scheme to date for a number of simple reasons:

1. He had a great reputation on Wall Street and was actually a legend for almost fifty years.
2. The returns claimed were modest but reliable. Even during significant market downturns, the returns continued. This appealed to investors' greed, and they ignored the old adage, "If it is too good to be true, it probably is."
3. Madoff was low key and mixed in all the right circles.
4. He played hard to get and turned down some investors. Some investors schemed for years before being granted entrance into his club. If he took your money, there was no need to ask questions.
5. If you needed your money back, redemptions were handled promptly with no questions asked.
6. Oversight was amazingly lax. The Securities and Exchange Commission (SEC) inquired at least eight times and never found anything significant.
7. Auditors were also incredibly lax.

As an example of how he was almost detected, an SEC auditor requested to see some records. While some of Madoff's employees distracted the auditor, others busily falsified what the auditor asked for. To hide the fact that the new records were just printed and still warm, the employees put them in the office refrigerator to cool them off![12]

The scheme finally collapsed during the 2008 financial crisis when Madoff ran out of cash to fulfill the redemption requests. Madoff turned himself and his two sons in to the authorities. While it is impossible to estimate the exact amount, he is estimated to have stolen over $17 billion from investors, including many charities.

---

12. James Sterngold, "Unraveling the Lies That Madoff Told," *Wall Street Journal, December 11, 2013, https://www.wsj.com/articles/no-headline-available-1386714437.*

Bernie Madoff, his wife and one of his sons tried to commit suicide. Bernie was sentenced to 150 years in prison, and many of his associates are serving time as well.

Most people know that knowingly filing a false tax return is a crime, but **tax cheating** is a very different type of crime. If you fail to pay your taxes, the government does not send out a tax bill to everybody else for your unpaid share. The amount of tax that is not paid by the tax fraudsters is paid by the honest taxpayers. It is easy for cheaters to believe that this is a victimless crime.

As long as there have been tax collectors there have been tax evaders. Archeologists have even found evidence of tax cheating from Babylonian days!

The most common belief as to why people cheat on their taxes is the cost-benefit Becker Rational Model, as summarized in Chart 2-1. According to IRS data, taxpayers rarely underreport wages, interest, dividend, stock or pension income since these are easy for the IRS to check up on. People who are paid in cash, however, cheat at about a ten times higher rate because they believe the risks of detection are much lower.[13] Add to this that only about 3,500 people in the United States are convicted of tax fraud and, as is illustrated in What Would You Do 3-8, the incentive to cheat is pretty obvious.

WHAT WOULD YOU DO 3-8

Double Dipping

Your friend is a surgeon who shares office costs with other physicians. While the medical office does the billing and gives her a check for his share, after costs, twice a month, your friend is responsible for paying all of her personal bills.

Fairly frequently your friend travels to conferences, which are paid from her corporation. She is reimbursed by the office for these costs which, over a year's period, are significant. Instead of putting the money in the corporate checkbook and crediting the amounts paid, she goes to the bank and cashes these checks. This money is then used for personal expenses. Your friend was audited once by the IRS and this never came up during the audit examination.

How do you feel about this scheme? Do the rewards exceed the potential pitfalls? If your friend asked your opinion, what would you advise?

---

13. Internal Revenue Service, *Tax Gap for Tax Year 2006, January 6, 2012, https://www.irs. gov/pub/newsroom/overview_tax_gap_2006.pdf.*

Discussion Questions

1. Of the various occupational frauds, which are the most disturbing to you? How can they be reduced or mitigated?

2. Distinguish between fraud and an error.

3. What is the fraud triangle? Why does each component have to be there in order to pull off a successful theft?

4. Which of the three components of the fraud triangle worry you the most? Why is that one more important than the others?

5. Why are small businesses more vulnerable to fraud? Compared to larger businesses, what signs of possible fraud might they find?

6. Do you think that the concept of materiality is incompatible with ethical behavior? Explain your answer.

7. What factors do you believe cause frauds to go undetected? What can be done about this?

8. Discuss three ways a chain of sporting goods stores might manipulate revenue or expense recognition. For each one of these, come up with a way to catch it before the fraud gets too far.

9. Why would a business want to improperly capitalize expenses? Won't the depreciation/amortization eventually catch up?

10. If you are the 100% owner of a business, is there anything wrong with "cookie jar" accounting? Why or why not?

11. Which are taxpayers more likely to cheat on: mortgage interest payments or charitable contributions? How about cash charitable contributions or non-cash contributions (such as clothes to Goodwill)? Why?

12. Your employer sells industrial equipment on account. At the end of the fiscal year, the company sold a piece of equipment to a customer for $400,000. You are surprised at this amount since the customer purchased the exact same piece of equipment a month earlier for $320,000.

Being a bit curious, you look at the fine print in the contract. Sure enough, it says that the customer is only liable for $320,000 if the invoice is paid within 60 days. This page of the agreement is not given to the auditors.

a. Should you record the sale at $400,000?
b. If your annual bonus was dependent on this sale, how would that influence your answer?
c. What controls should be in place to catch this sort of scheme?

13. You work for an entertainment company with two identical intangible assets. Each asset has a cost of $50,000 and a fair value of $75,000. The company sells one of the assets at the end of the fiscal year for $110,000 and executes a separate side agreement to sell the second asset to the same buyer the following year for $40,000. Viewed together, the two agreements total the intangible asset value of $150,000.

a. What is the effect on net income in each of the two years?
b. Is there anything wrong with this transaction? Why or why not?
c. If you stumbled on the paperwork, what would you do?

Case Study[14]

In the 1980s, poor management and outright fraud required a $300 billion bailout by Washington of US savings and loan associations. The biggest failure was a $2.5 billion bailout of California-based Lincoln Savings, led by Charles Keating. Lincoln Savings & Loan became the poster child of a much larger culture of financial abuse in the "go-go" period of the 1980s.

---

14. Bill Hewitt, Jane Sims Podesta, and Kathy Shocket, "Financier Charles Keating Is the $2 Billion Man of the Savings and Loan Crisis," *People.com, December 04, 1989, http://people.com/archive/financier-charles-keating-is-the-2-billion-man-of-the-savings-and-loan-crisis-vol-32-no-23/.*

Keating bought Lincoln Savings & Loan for $51 million in 1984 and almost immediately the bank began to make aggressive investing bets with depositors' money, including stocks, junk bonds and real estate ventures. By 1987, Lincoln's assets had gone from $1 billion to $3.9 billion; however, an audit revealed that the bank had $135 million of unreported losses and was more than $600 million above a federally mandated cap on risky savings and loan investments.

In 1987, Keating persuaded five US senators—to whose campaigns he had contributed a total of $1.3 million—to intervene on his behalf when federal bank regulators first began investigating his financial dealings. When asked if this bought him influence, Keating responded, "I certainly hope so." By doing this, he was able to get the FBI, the SEC and other regulatory agencies to back off their investigations into Lincoln. The group of senators later became known collectively as the "Keating Five."

While Lincoln's reported assets grew to as large as $5.4 billion, investors subsequently discovered that the company continued to have non-reported losses. Lincoln filed for bankruptcy in 1989, and many of its 23,000 customers lost their entire life savings. US taxpayers were forced to pay $3.4 billion to help cover the bank's losses.

The government case against Keating involved allegations that he recklessly invested Lincoln savings funds in speculative ventures, including undeveloped real estate and junk bonds, many of which went sour. They also looked at accusations that Keating siphoned off as much as $95 million from Lincoln into another company, from which he and his family then took some $34 million in salaries, bonuses and stock sales. When called before the House Banking Committee, Keating refused to answer any questions.

On December 4, 1991, Keating was convicted in California on 73 counts of wire and bankruptcy fraud and sentenced him to 12 years of prison. After serving 50 months, Keating's conviction was overturned on a technicality.[15] He died in March 2014.

---

15. United States Court of Appeals, Ninth Circuit, United States of America, Plaintiff-Appellant, v. Charles H. Keating, Jr., Charles H. Keating, III, Defendants-Appellees, June 09, 1998, Nos 97-50049, 97-50056.

Case Study Questions

1. Considering Keatings answer to the reporter's question, do you believe contacting the senators was ethical? If you were his advisor, would you have suggested that he testify to the House Banking Committee? Why would you recommend this action?

2. Given these circumstances, do you feel that Keating's sentence was appropriate? Why do you feel this way?

3. Lincoln Savings & Loan was a prime example of financial abuse during the 1980s. Why do you think they got away with this for so long? Do you think it can be done again today?

CHAPTER 4

FEDERAL LEGAL ISSUES IN ETHICS

"The clearest way to show what the rule of law means to us in everyday life is to recall what has happened when there is no rule of law."

—*Dwight D. Eisenhower, 34th president of the United States (1890–1969)*

Accounting has a long history, going back hundreds of years when double-entry bookkeeping was first invented in Italy. Until the early twentieth century, it was left mostly to the private sector to provide reliable financial information to their owners and investors.

Then came the 1929 stock market crash and the Great Depression. Some of the blame was attributed to inadequate, and sometimes misleading, accounting and reporting. While many of the rules that apply to CPAs are set by the individual states, in this chapter we will discuss these federal legal issues in accounting:

- Standard setting
- Statutory (legal) liability

- Securities laws
- Dodd Frank Act
- Whistleblowing

Public Accounting Standard Setting

The pressures caused by the Great Depression caused the accounting profession to establish standards. In addition to this, Congress acted by passing the **Securities Act of 1933** and the **Securities Exchange Act of 1934**, which were designed to restore investor confidence in the public markets. The Securities Act of 1933 requires certain accounting and disclosure requirements for an initial public offering of stocks and bonds while the Securities Exchange Act of 1934 sets certain accounting requirements for the stock markets.

Just as importantly, the 1934 Act created the **US Securities and Exchange Commission (SEC)**. This governmental body was given the power and responsibility of setting financial accounting and reporting standards for publicly traded companies. The SEC may also choose to delegate these responsibilities to the private sector. If the SEC does not agree with a specific standard issued by the private sector, the SEC may set their own rule, which it has done many times.

The very first private-sector standard-setting body, the **Committee on Accounting Procedure** (CAP) was initially a committee of the AICPA. From 1938 to 1959, the CAP issued fifty-one **Accounting Research Bulletins** (ARBs). They focused on making specific rules rather than taking a conceptual approach, which made the CAP subject to criticism.

From 1959 to 1973, the CAP was replaced by the **Accounting Principles Board** (APB), who issued thirty-one Accounting Principles Board Opinions (APBs), four statements and several interpretations of accounting standards. APB Statement No. 4 tried to establish a conceptual framework but failed. In addition to this unsuccessful effort, the APB was criticized for its lack of independence and for not having diverse interest groups participating in the process.

In 1973, a new organization, the **Financial Accounting Standards Board** (FASB), replaced the APB. The FASB has seven full-time members representing the accounting profession, industry and other various interest groups, such as the government and accounting educators. In 1984, the **Government Accounting Standards Board** (GASB) was established to issue standards for government financial reporting. These two bodies are still in operation.

The United States is not alone when it comes to accounting standards. In 1973, the International Accounting Standards Committee (IASC) was formed, which was the predecessor of the current international standard-setting body, the **International Accounting Standards Board** (IASB). The IASB has no authority to enforce compliance with their standards and its adoption is voluntary. Since 2002, the IASB and FASB have worked to remove the many differences between international standards and US GAAP with the ultimate goal of a common set of global accounting standards. While some of the projects have been successfully completed, others have been discontinued because the two boards could not agree on key issues.

Legal Liability of Accountants

Common-law liability requires a CPA to perform professional services with due care. This means if a CPA performs a job with the same degree of skill and judgment possessed by others in the profession, he or she will have met this standard and cannot be held liable for errors. What Would You Do 4-1 demonstrates how an error might be handled.

WHAT WOULD YOU DO 4-1
Cash Won't Balance

You are the outside CPA of a hospital. Part of your duties is to reconcile co-payments from patients and their families to what was deposited in the bank and to the general ledger. You are very careful and always balance to the penny. Or so you thought.

One Friday before a holiday weekend it was particularly busy and, as usual, at the end of the day, you balance the cash. This time, however, you find that the balance is exactly $1,000 short from what was expected. Since it is Friday afternoon, there is nobody in the office to call and the financial statements are due on Monday morning. Perhaps there is a reasonable explanation, but you need to do some research in order to discover what it may be. In order to understand the mystery, you attempt to contact the cashier, who, naturally, just left for the long weekend.

If you report the shortage, the cashier most likely will be terminated. If you do not reflect the shortage on the financial statements, they will be misleading. How would you handle this delicate situation?

Breach of contract is a claim that the CPA did not perform services in accordance with the terms of their contract or, in public accounting, the engagement letter. Although CPAs may have a signed engagement letter with their client, frequently a third party, such as a bank or a disgruntled investor, might sue a CPA for not exercising the appropriate level of professional care. When this happens, they will not only sue for breach of contract but also anything else they can think of, like deceit and fraud.

Case 4-1

CD LISTENING BAR[1]

CD Listening Bar operates retail stores specializing in prerecorded music. Under the name Super Discount CDs & DVDs, they also are a worldwide wholesaler of music and movies in all formats. As business expanded, CD Listening Bar experienced growing pains; its accounting software was inadequate and needed to be upgraded.

McGladrey & Pullen, a national accounting firm and an independent reseller of Great Plains Software, offered to provide software "implementation, installation, training and continuing support" to CD Listening Bar, and both parties signed an engagement letter incorporating the proposal. They also signed a "Master Software License Agreement" for the use of the Great Plains accounting software that specified that the parties to the license agreement were Great Plains and CD Listening Bar, not the accounting firm.

In its lawsuit, CD Listening Bar said that the accounting firm failed to install the software in "a prompt, workmanlike" manner, and eventually "walked off the job and abandoned" the client without completing the installation. CD Listening Bar was awarded $2 million for, among other things, breach of contract.

Sometimes a third party will claim that they have a **privity relationship** with a client, which is a relationship between two parties recognized by law. Obviously, one of the parties will be the client while the other is the CPA, so there is no question of privity between the two of them. There may also be foreseen, and reasonably foreseeable, third parties who may rely on the work. Each state has its

---

1. CD Listening Bar, Inc. v. McGladrey & Pullen, Court of Appeal, Fourth District, Division 3, California, December 28, 2001, No. G029317, re Super.Ct.No. OOCCI4372.

own rules but the majority of states follow what is known as the "modified privity requirement."[2] This rule allows nonclients to sue CPAs provided that: (1) the client belongs to a "limited group"; and (2) the CPA had actual knowledge that their work would be supplied to that group.

In California, this legal rule is a bit more complicated:

1. In cases of **ordinary negligence** (failure to act in a reasonably prudent manner), the CPA has *no duty* to third parties.
2. In **negligent misrepresentation** (honestly believing that the work is true but without reasonable ground for such belief), the CPA has a duty to third parties who would be *known with substantial certainty* to rely on the misrepresentation.
3. In cases of **intentional misrepresentation** (the work was false or reckless without knowledge of the truth), the CPA owes a duty to third parties who could be *reasonably foreseen* to rely on the misrepresentation.

Case 4-2

BILY V. ARTHUR YOUNG[3]

Osborne Computer Company hired Arthur Young & Company to audit their financial statements. The audit firm gave unqualified or "clean" audit opinions on Osborne's financial statements for two years. Bily and others, who were not clients of Young, invested in Osborne based on the audit findings. According to the suit, Osborne's liabilities were actually $3 million greater than what the audit report showed.

The jury, relying on the concept of negligent misrepresentation, ruled against the accounting firm and awarded $4.3 million of damages to Bily.

Securities Act of 1933

The Securities Act of 1933 regulates the disclosure of information in a registration statement for a new public offering of securities (an **IPO**).[4] CPAs who

---

2. *Restatement (Second) of the Law of Torts, §552 (Washington D.C.: The American Law Institute, 1976)*
3. Bily v. Arthur Young, California 1992, 834 P. 2d. 745.
4. Securities Exchange Act of 1933, Title 15 of the US Code.

assist in the preparation of the registration statement can be found civilly liable if the registration statement: (1) contains false statements of material facts; (2) omits material facts; or (3) omits information that, if not given, makes the facts on the statement misleading. Unless the purchase was made after one year from the offering, there is no need to prove you relied on the financial statements, just that one of the factors is true.

A CPA might say that the information is not **material.** The SEC and the courts define material as the kind of information that an average prudent investor would want to have so they can make an intelligent, informed decision whether or not to buy the stock. In other words, had the investor known the truth, they might not have purchased the stock. Of course, minor errors are not material. An example of materiality is illustrated in What Would You Do 4-2.

WHAT WOULD YOU DO 4-2

A New Millionaire

You are taking a ride with your friend in her expensive new car, purchased with the proceeds of her medical device company IPO. She takes you by the company headquarters and is proud to say that she owns the building and is leasing it back to the company at a pretty nice profit. When you ask what the underwriters and auditors thought of the arrangement, she looked at you a bit puzzled and answered, "They never asked, so why should I tell them?"

Do you believe this is something that should have been disclosed as part of the IPO? If so, what would you advise your friend? If you believe it was not necessary to disclose, explain why.

Another defense of a CPA may be to say they exercised **due diligence.** This means the CPA performed a reasonable investigation of the financial statements and had no reason to believe they were false or misleading. The test is if a prudent person would have made a similar investigation under similar circumstances.

Case 4-3

CRAZY EDDIE[5]

In New York during the 1980s, Eddie Antar advertised that his prices were lower than the competition. There were funny, clever commercials that made the Crazy Eddie store famous and his business boomed.

From 1984 through 1987, Crazy Eddie made several public stock offerings. The prospectuses gave the impression that the business was a going concern, but there were a number of significant errors on the financial statements, including inflated inventory and net income. Some of the stock buyers sued the company and the auditor for failing to uncover the fraudulent and fake activities. They were able to show they suffered a loss by relying on the registration statements. Note that they were investors, not clients.

Based on the Securities Act of 1933, they did not have to prove fraud or gross negligence, only that the material errors in the registration statements were misleading and they lost money. The auditor was unable to prove that they exercised due professional care and lost the case.

Securities Exchange Act of 1934

While the Securities Act of 1933 relates to IPOs, the Securities Exchange Act of 1934 regulates reporting by public companies, generally those who are listed and traded on stock exchanges. Most entities with assets of $10 million or more and 500 or more stockholders must register, plus file quarterly (10-Q) and annual reports (10-K). In addition, whenever a significant event takes place, they must also file a Form 8-K.

The SEC has various regulations, plus **Financial Reporting Releases** and **Staff Accounting Bulletins**. The regulations, plus these two unofficial documents, provide interpretations of the law plus rules describing who must file.

Section 18 of the Act makes a person who makes a material **false or misleading statement** liable if it is contained in a document filed with the SEC, while the liability of CPAs and auditors is based on **Rule 10**. This rule makes it illegal

5. Securities and Exchange Commission v. Eddie Antar, Sam E. Antar, Mitchell Antar, Isaac Keirey, David Panoff, Eddie Gindi, and Kathleen Morin, February 10, 1997, Civil Action No. 89-773, Litigation Release 15251.

for a CPA to: (1) employ any device, scheme, or artifice to defraud; (2) make an untrue statement of a material fact or omit a material fact necessary in order to make the statement, in light of the circumstances under which they were made, not misleading; or (3) engage in any act, practice or course of business to commit fraud or deceit in connection with the purchase or sale of the security.[6]

Case 4-4

ERNST & ERNST V. HOCHFELDER[7]

The president of a publicly traded brokerage firm recommended that Hochfelder invest in securities that the president represented would provide a high rate of return; the president then took the money and used it for his personal use. The fraud was discovered after the president committed suicide, leaving a note that the brokerage was bankrupt and the accounts were nonexistent.

The suit against the auditor said Ernst & Ernst did not use "appropriate auditing procedures" and should have discovered the fraud; thus, the financial statements were misleading, and Hochfelder sued under the Securities Act of 1934.

The rule at the brokerage was that nobody other than the president could open mail, even if he was away. Hochfelder said that, had the auditor conducted a proper audit, it would have discovered this mail rule, a material weakness that would have led them to the embezzlement.

The Supreme Court said that a private suit for damages was not allowed. Rule 10 is not about negligence but, rather, willful conduct designed to deceive investors, which was clearly not the case here. While there may have been audit deficiencies, the Securities Exchange Act of 1934 punishes only *willful* conduct designed to deceive or defraud investors.

In a footnote, the Supreme Court said that, in certain areas of law, recklessness may be the same as intentional, and that gross negligence (discussed in Chapter 5) might be enough to sue under this statute.

---

6. Code of Federal Regulations, Title 17, Chapter 11, Section 240.10b-5, *Employment of manipulative and deceptive devices.*
7. US Supreme Court, 425 US 185, *Ernst & Ernst v. Hochfelder*, March 30, 1976, No. 74-1042, 425 US 185.

SEC Enforcement[8]

In FY 2017, the SEC opened 754 enforcement actions. A significant number of the Commission's cases concerned investment advisory issues, securities offerings, and issuer reporting/accounting and auditing, each being about 20% of the overall number of actions. They also brought actions relating to market manipulation, insider trading, and broker-dealers, with each comprising about 10% of the overall number of actions.

These were just the number of new cases; in FY 2017, the SEC ordered $2.9 billion in disgorgement of ill-gotten gains. There were also penalties imposed of $832 million. As in most years, a significant percentage of the dollar value of disgorgement and penalties were large amounts from a small number of cases.

In FY 2017, 73% of the Commission's enforcement actions involved charges against one or more individuals. There were over 625 bars and suspensions of wrongdoers in FY 2017. Some examples are listed here:

—The accounting firm of Ernst & Young LLP agreed to pay more than $11.8 million to settle claims related to failed audits of an oil services company that used deceptive income tax accounting to inflate earnings. In addition, two of the firm's partners agreed to suspension from practicing before the Commission[9].

—KPMG LLP and an audit partner were penalized for failing to properly audit the financial statements of an oil and gas company, resulting in investors being misinformed about the value. The firm agreed to pay more than $6.2 million to settle the charges, and the audit partner agreed to a two-year suspension from appearing and practicing before the Commission[10].

—Penn West Petroleum Ltd., a Canadian-based oil and gas company, and three of its former top finance executives were penalized for their roles in an extensive, multi-year accounting fraud. One of them agreed to a permanent suspension from appearing and practicing before the SEC as an accountant,

---

8. US Securities and Exhange Commission, *Division of Enforcement 2017 Annual Report*, accessed May 25, 2018, *https://www.sec.gov/files/enforcement-annual-report-2017.pdf.*

9. U.S. Securities and Exchange Commission, *Ernst & Young to Pay $11.8 Million for Audit Failures*, October 18, 2016, *https://www.sec.gov/news/pressrelease/2016-219.html*

10. U.S. Securities and Exchange Commission, *SEC Charges KPMG with Audit Failures*, August 12, 2017 *https://www.sec.gov/news/press-release/2017-142*

which includes not participating in the financial reporting or audits of public companies. The other two are in litigation, with the SEC seeking permanent injunctions and monetary relief, officer-and-director bars, and a clawback of incentive-based compensation awarded to one of them[11].

In other words, the SEC has significant enforcement powers and is not shy about exercising them.

The Dodd-Frank Wall Street Reform and Consumer Protection Act

The **Dodd-Frank Wall Street Reform Act** was passed in 2010 as a direct result of the Great Recession. The goal of this law is to provide consumer protection and restrictions on the activities of organizations and businesses that provide financial services. The law does this through a variety of means.

The law set up **a Financial Stability Oversight Council** that identifies risks affecting the financial product industry. It also oversees financial firms other than banks, like hedge funds, and recommends that the government, under the auspices of the Federal Reserve, supervise any that get too big. They do this requiring the firm to increase their reserve requirement, with the goal of preventing them from becoming "too big to fail."

What has commonly been called the **Volcker Rule** bans banks from using or owning hedge funds for their own profit. It also does not allow banks to use their depositors' funds to trade on the banks' accounts, and it basically gave banks seven years to get out of the hedge fund business entirely.

Dodd-Frank also gives regulators the power to regulate some of the most dangerous derivatives, like credit default swaps (one of the major causes of the recession). By identifying excessive risk-taking, this can be brought to policy-makers' attention before a major crisis occurs. It also ensures derivative trades are transacted in public.

Hedge funds must now be registered with the SEC; prior to the law they were unregulated. They must provide data about their trades and portfolios so the SEC can assess overall market risk, giving states more information to help regulate them.

---

11. U.S. Securities and Exchange Commission, *SEC Charges Oil and Gas Company and Top Finance Executives with Accounting Fraud, June 28, 2017, https://www.sec.gov/news/press-release/2017-120*

Prior to this bill, investors trusted the credit rating agencies, like Moody's and Standard & Poor's, at least until they realized that many of the derivatives and mortgage-based securities were overrated. There is now an **Office of Credit Ratings** at the SEC that regulates these credit ratings.

The **Consumer Financial Protection Bureau** (CFPB) was created to oversee credit reporting agencies, plus credit and debit cards, payday and consumer loans (other than auto loans made by dealers). Other functions are to regulate credit, mortgage and bank fees, set rules to help homeowners understand their loans, and require banks to verify borrower's income, credit history and job status.

Another new federal agency, the **Federal Insurance Office**, identifies insurance companies that create a risk for the entire system by gathering information about the insurance industry. It also makes sure affordable insurance is available to minorities and other underserved communities.

Finally, Dodd-Frank gave the **Government Accountability Office** new powers. It can review future emergency loans when needed, and the Treasury Department must now approve any new emergency loans.

Case 4-5

CONSUMER FINANCIAL PROTECTION BUREAU V. GOLDEN VALLEY LENDING, INC., SILVER CLOUD FINANCIAL, INC., MOUNTAIN SUMMIT FINANCIAL, INC., AND MAJESTIC LAKE FINANCIAL, INC.[12]

The Consumer Financial Protection Bureau took action against four online lenders for deceiving consumers. The CFPB alleged that the lenders made deceptive demands and illegally took money from consumer bank accounts for debts that consumers did not legally owe. They seek to stop the unlawful practices, recoup relief for harmed consumers, and impose a penalty. Their investigation showed that the high-cost loans violated licensing requirements or interest-rate caps, or both, that made the loans void in whole or in part in at least seventeen states. The specific allegations include the following:

---

12. Consumer Financial Protection Bureau, "CFPB Sues Four Online Lenders for Collecting on Debts Consumers Did Not Legally Owe, *ConsumerFinance.org, April 27, 2017, https://www.consumerfinance.gov/about-us/newsroom/cfpb-sues-four-online-lenders-collecting-debts-consumers-did-not-legally-owe/.*

Deceiving consumers about loan payments that were not owed: The lenders pursued consumers for payments even though the loans were void under state law and, thus, payments could not legally be collected. The interest rates the lenders charged were high enough to violate usury laws in some states where they did business, and violation of these usury laws also made the loans void. In addition, the lenders did not obtain licenses to lend or collect in some states. The four lenders created the false impression that they had a legal right to collect payments and that consumers had a legal obligation to pay off the loans, even though this was not true.

Collecting loan payments that consumers did not owe: The four lenders made electronic withdrawals from consumers' bank accounts or called or sent letters to consumers demanding payment for debts that consumers were under no legal obligation to pay.

Failing to disclose the real cost of credit: The lenders' websites did not disclose the annual percentage rates that applied to the loans. When contacted by prospective borrowers, the lenders' representatives also did not tell consumers the annual percentage rate that would apply to the loans.

The law created the **Public Company Accounting Standards Board**, also known as the PCASB. Most of the standards for this area of the law cover auditing of publicly traded companies, which is covered in Chapter 5.

Whistleblowing

Whistleblowing is when somebody discloses to others an action that violates the organization's policies or the law. This can be used either within the company (such as using a hotline or informing an internal auditor) or outside the company (such as telling the external auditors or going directly to the newspapers or the SEC).

Section 922 of the Dodd-Frank Act[13] allows the SEC to pay awards to eligible whistleblowers who voluntarily provide the SEC with original information that leads to a successful enforcement action yielding monetary sanctions of over $1 million. The award is between 10% and 30% of the total monetary sanctions collected in either an SEC or any related action, such as in a criminal

---

13. US Securities and Exchange Commission, "Whistleblower Program," August 12, 2011, https://www.sec.gov/spotlight/dodd-frank/whistleblower.shtml.

case. Since it began in 2011, the SEC's whistleblower program has paid out more than $1 billion.

The act also expressly prohibits retaliation by employers against whistleblowers. Should there be retaliation, the whistleblower can sue if they are discharged or discriminated against by their employers.

According to a recent survey,[14] reporting of suspected wrongdoing in US organizations has reached a historic high, while rates of retaliation for reporting of suspected wrongdoing have doubled in the last two years. Other findings include the following:

- 69% of employees said they reported misconduct they observed, a 19% increase and all-time high since the inception of the study.
- When asked if employees had experienced retaliation for reporting, 44% of respondents said they had been retaliated against, compared to 22% five years earlier.
- Historically, the survey found that reporting and retaliation rise and fall together; however, in the latest study, retaliation rose significantly higher than reporting.
- Rates of observed misconduct have declined 15% since 2013, close to the historic low.
- 16% of employees experienced pressure to compromise ethical standards, a 23% increase since 2013. 84% of the same employees also observed misconduct.
- 20% of employees say their company has a strong ethical culture, which is thought to be the most important strategy for minimizing wrongdoing. 40% of employees believe their company has a weak or weak leaning ethical culture, a trend that has not notably changed since 2000.

Research shows that whistleblowers hope (and believe) their speaking out will correct the organizational wrongdoing, but few are ready to "blow the whistle." The major reason they do not do anything is that, despite assurances to the

---

14. Ethics and Compliance Initiative, "Global Workplace Survey: US Rates of Reported Misconduct Sets National Record; Retaliation Has Doubled," March 19, 2018, https://connects.ethics.org/blogs/eci-connector/2018/03/19/us-reported-misconduct-sets-national-record.

contrary, they are afraid they will be retaliated against.[15] What Would You Do 4-3 gives an example of how to handle this tricky situation.

WHAT WOULD YOU DO 4-3

The Airplane

A publicly held company you work for owns several aircraft, including propeller planes and luxury jets. In compiling the information for the annual income tax returns, you notice a donation to an obscure charity of a twenty-year-old plane. You know the plane was not in great shape, so you are blown away that an outside appraisal of this junk-heap shows that it is worth $97,500. You even remember your boss laughing that it would be amazing if it could even be flown to the charity without crashing but, in any event, he had insurance.

Should you say something? What are your options? Of those options, which would you most likely choose?

Case 4-6

LANCE ARMSTRONG[16]

Lance Armstrong was stripped of his seven Tour de France titles for doping violations. Most people don't realize that the second-place finishers in six of those races were also suspended for doping at various times in their careers.

Lance Armstrong's former teammate, Floyd Landis, himself an admitted doper, sued Armstrong and his team on behalf of the United States Postal Service, which sponsored the team. Landis claimed USPS's contracts with Armstrong's team prohibited the team from violating cycling's rules about drugs and doping, and that when they violated those rules, they also violated the law. The government agreed with Landis and joined the suit, demanding Armstrong return the money the USPS had paid.

---

15. Janet P. Near and Marcia P. Miceli, "Effective Whistle-Blowing," *The Academy of Management Review* 20, no. 3 (July 1995): 679–708.

16. Phillips & Cohen LLP, "Lance Armstrong's $5M Settlement of Whistleblower Case Sends Message," *Whistleblower Law Insights*, April 20, 2018, *https://www.phillipsandcohen.com/68304-2/*.

Armstrong's defense wasn't that he didn't cheat; he even told Oprah Winfrey and her audience that he did. Instead, his main defense was that the government wasn't harmed.

With the trial less than a month away, both Armstrong and the government saw the risks of trial and settled for $5 million. Since these matters are, by law, confidential, it was not disclosed if Landis received any whistleblower compensation; however, based on the law, he would be entitled to an award.

Discussion Questions

1. What is common law liability? How is that different from statutory liability?

2. What is the difference between an error and negligence? Give some examples.

3. What actions might cause a CPA to be sued under the Securities Act of 1933?

4. How can one distinguish the difference between actually foreseen third-party users and reasonably foreseeable third-party users?

5. Under what circumstances can a third party sue a CPA under the Securities Exchange Act of 1934?

6. Identify the most important provisions for CPAs in the Dodd-Frank Act. How might the threat of penalties change the way companies do business?

7. Have you, or do you know somebody who, found wrongdoing at a company? What actions were taken and why? Looking back at what was done, was that the right call?

8. Why do you think some corporate scam artists gravitate to public companies? What do you think can be done about it?

9. Why do some believe that a violation of organizational ethics is an internal organizational issue? How might you respond to this?

10. Just because a person has a right to blow the whistle, does that mean they have a duty to do so? How did you come to this conclusion?

11. You are hired as the president of a nonprofit organization with six employees. Once on the job, you learn that three of them are closely related (mother, daughter and nephew). Since it is a small organization, there are few effective internal controls. You also notice how the three of them seem to spend a lot of time huddled and do not seem to want to share their work with others.

   a. Is this something that should be brought up to the board of directors? What factors come into play when making this decision?
   b. Assume the annual audit comes and goes with the external auditors not even inquiring about any family-related party issues. Should you have brought this issue up to the auditors before the audit report was issued? If so, what should you do now?
   c. What ramifications might there be to your job based on the answers to questions 11a and 11b?

Case Study[17]

While working as director of the Technical Accounting Research and Training in the Finance and Accounting Department at Halliburton, Anthony Menendez raised concerns internally about questionable accounting practices. Menendez disclosed to his supervisor that Halliburton's revenue recognition principles did not conform with generally accepted accounting principles. Menendez's supervisor initially responded by telling Menendez that he was not a "team player" and should try harder to work with colleagues to resolve accounting issues.

After Halliburton failed to address his concerns, Menendez filed a confidential disclosure with the SEC about Halliburton's accounting practices. In addition, Menendez sent a memo to Halliburton's board of directors raising the same issues he disclosed to the SEC, and that memo was forwarded to Halliburton's general counsel. When Halliburton received a notice of investigation from the

---

17. Jason Zuckerman, "Fifth Circuit Holds That "Outing" a Whistleblower Is an Adverse Action under SOX," *Zuckermanlaw.com, January 26, 2018, https://www.zuckermanlaw.com/ circuit-holds-outing-whistleblower-adverse-action-sox/. Also, United States Court of Appeals for the Fifth Circuit, Petition for Review of the Final Decision and Order of the United States Department of Labor Administrative Review Board, November 12, 2014, no. 13-60323.*

SEC requiring Halliburton to retain documents, Halliburton's counsel inferred from Menendez's internal disclosures that he was the source of the SEC inquiry.

After being outed as a whistleblower, Menendez's colleagues began treating him differently, refusing to work and associate with him. Halliburton granted his request for paid administrative leave, and within a year, Menendez resigned and sued.

The main issue on appeal was whether Menendez suffered an "adverse action" when Halliburton disclosed his identity as a whistleblower. The court concluded that Halliburton's outing of a whistleblower to his colleagues "created an environment of ostracism" for the whistleblower, which well might dissuade a reasonable employee from whistleblowing in the future.

Menendez was awarded $30,000. Halliburton was never penalized by the SEC.

Case Study Questions

1. Do you believe that Halliburton, or its employees, should have also been penalized? Why do you feel this way?

2. Menendez was awarded a fairly small amount for putting himself and his family through years of litigation. While he did eventually get a job at another public company, do you think being labeled as a whistleblower and a disloyal employee was worth it?

3. The facts of this case have nothing with somebody stealing money from Halliburton but, rather, moving a fairly small amount of revenue from one accounting period to an earlier period. There is no tax fraud or cheating of customers or their employees; the only ramification to the company was on cash flow for paying taxes a bit earlier. Given this and all of the other facts in the case, what would you do in a similar situation?

CHAPTER 5

ACCOUNTING ETHICS

"Have the courage to say no. Have the courage to face the truth. Do the right thing because it is right. These are the magic keys to living your life with integrity."

—W. Clement Stone, businessman, philanthropist, author (1902—2002)

L ike most professional occupations, the accounting profession faces its own set of ethical issues. The AICPA, PCAOB, SEC, and many CPA societies have created their own set of guiding principles and rules. In this chapter we will discuss the following:

- AICPA Code of Professional Conduct
- AICPA Rules of Professional Conduct
- PCAOB rules for auditors
- Enforcement

Principles of Professional Conduct: Basic Framework

The AICPA and many CPA societies' ethics rules recognize the profession's responsibilities to the public, clients and colleagues, no matter if the CPA is in public or private accounting. They guide CPAs in the performance of their role and express the basic tenets of ethical and professional conduct. Note that, while these rules are written for members of the AICPA, most state boards of accountancy follow them as well. In addition, many courts use these as the minimum standards of work done by CPAs.

The basic framework of ethical conduct consists of:[1]

- responsibilities (Chart 5-1);
- the public interest (Chart 5-2);
- integrity (Chart 5-3);
- objectivity and independence (Chart 5-4);
- due care (Chart 5-5); and
- scope and nature of services (Chart 5-6).

Chart 5-1

RESPONSIBILITIES

In carrying out their responsibilities as professionals, members[2] should exercise sensitive professional and moral judgments in all their activities. (AICPA Code of Professional Conduct §300.010.01)

No matter if you are a physician, attorney or a CPA, professionals perform an essential role in society. Consistent with that role, CPAs have **responsibilities** to those who use their professional services. There is also a duty to cooperate with other CPAs to improve the accounting practices and standards, maintain the public's confidence, and carry out the profession's responsibilities for self-governance.

Based on §300.010.01, the collective efforts of all AICPA members are required to maintain and enhance the traditions of the profession. What Would You Do 5-1 illustrates a practical dilemma.

---

1. All definitions of the principles and rules in these charts are from the applicable sections of the *AICPA Code of Professional Conduct, found at https://www.aicpa.org/research/standards/codeofconduct.html.*
2. AICPA members

WHAT WOULD YOU DO 5-1

Joining the AICPA

The CPA firm you work for insists that the partners join the AICPA; for all other staff members the firm does not encourage membership, nor will it pay dues if they join. The partners feel that the AICPA only looks out for the biggest firms, and the only reason the partners are members is to get the insurance benefits.

Do you agree with this attitude? Is it right to join and pay dues just for the insurance benefits, or should you be more involved? In this situation, would you join and pay the dues yourself? Why?

Chart 5-2

THE PUBLIC INTEREST

Members should accept the obligation to act in a way that will serve the public interest, honor the public trust, and demonstrate a commitment to professionalism. (AICPA Code of Professional Conduct §300.030.01)

The accounting profession's duty is to clients, credit grantors, governments, employers, investors, the business and financial community and others who rely on the objectivity and integrity of CPAs. The **public interest** is defined as the collective well-being of the community of people and institutions that the profession serves.

CPAs often come across conflicting pressures. In resolving these conflicts, a CPA should act with integrity, meaning that clients' and/or employers' interests are best served. CPAs are expected to provide quality services, enter into fair fee arrangements, and offer a range of services in a manner that demonstrates a level of professionalism. What Would You Do 5-2 presents an interesting predicament.

WHAT WOULD YOU DO 5-2

Politics

You are a CPA who is responsible for expense reimbursements to a politician who flies home every weekend. Over the last few months, you notice that the "incidental costs" for each trip are increasing. In looking carefully at the receipts, you notice that cigars are being charged to the account. You ask the politician, who says that they are gifts to constituents and not to worry about it.

On one hand, the receipts are there and the expense is documented; on the other hand, you do not believe he is bringing cigars to constituents every trip, especially since the politician is a cigar smoker.

How would you handle this situation?

Chart 5-3

INTEGRITY

To maintain and broaden public confidence, members should perform all professional responsibilities with the highest sense of integrity. (AICPA Code of Professional Conduct §300.040.01)

Integrity is the quality of being honest and having strong moral principles. According to the standards, integrity is measured in terms of what is right and just. In the absence of specific rules, standards, or guidance or in the face of conflicting opinions, a CPA should make decisions by asking, "Am I doing what a person of integrity would do? Have I retained my integrity?" This requires the CPA to observe both the form and the spirit of technical and ethical standards.

Integrity is the benchmark against which a CPA must ultimately base all decisions. It requires a CPA to be, among other things, honest and candid while maintaining confidentiality. Professional services should never be subordinated to a CPA's personal gain or advantage. An inadvertent error and honest difference of opinion would not compromise integrity; as discussed in What Would You Do 5-3, deceit or subordination of principle certainly would.

WHAT WOULD YOU DO 5-3

Bad News

Your long-term client is a great guy who owns three retail furniture outlets. You have known him for a number of years, professionally as well as personally, and you really like him.

In preparing his tax returns, you see that, due to an increase in inventory at the end of the year, and after all expenses have been accounted for, he will be owing a substantial amount of taxes. Since all of his cash is tied up in inventory, he will probably be short when it comes time to pay. His wife just moved out and he has two children in college, so he is sort of distracted, financially and otherwise.

You really don't want to hurt the guy, but he does owe the taxes. How and when would you broach the news?

Chart 5-4

OBJECTIVITY AND INDEPENDENCE

A member should maintain objectivity and be free of conflicts of interest in discharging professional responsibilities. A member in public practice should be independent in fact and appearance when providing auditing and other attestation services. (AICPA Code of Professional Conduct §300.050.01)

Objectivity means to be impartial, intellectually honest, and free of conflicts of interest. **Independence** means that a CPA should avoid relationships that may appear, either in fact or appearance, to impair objectivity.

CPAs often have, even within the same client, multiple, and sometimes conflicting, interests; they must maintain objectivity in all of these roles. For example, CPAs in public practice perform audit, tax, and management advisory services. CPAs can prepare financial statements while working for others, perform internal auditing services, and serve in financial and management capacities in industry, education, and government. They also teach and train future CPAs at a college or university. Regardless of what they do, CPAs must protect the integrity of their work, maintain objectivity, and avoid any subordination of their judgment.

CPAs who are employees and prepare financial statements or perform tax or consulting services are expected to be just as objective. They must be scrupulous in their application of generally accepted accounting principles and candid in all their dealings with CPAs in public practice. What Would You Do 5-4 discusses how this might be handled in a practical setting.

WHAT WOULD YOU DO 5-4

The Best Price

Lauren Smith is the outside CPA for Sports Central, a chain of sporting goods stores. She has been asked to recommend a site for a new store. Lauren has an uncle who owns a shopping plaza in the area of town where the new store is to be located, so she decides to contact her uncle about leasing space in his plaza. Lauren also contacted several other shopping plazas and malls, but her uncle's store turned out to be the most economical place to lease.

Lauren is thinking about recommending locating the new store in her uncle's shopping plaza. How would you advise Laura to handle this situation?

Chart 5-5

DUE CARE

A member should observe the profession's technical and ethical standards, strive continually to improve competence and the quality of services, and discharge professional responsibility to the best of the member's ability. (AICPA Code of Professional Conduct §300.060.01)

Due care means doing the job with competence and diligence. It is the obligation to do the job to the best of your ability, while also watching out for the best interests of those for whom the services are performed.

Competence comes from a combination of education and experience. It begins with knowing what is required to become a CPA and, of course, passing the exam and meeting state licensing requirements. Remaining competent entails continuing education, staying up-to-date with pronouncements and general professional improvement. In all engagements and in all responsibilities, the CPA should try to achieve a level of competence that will ensure the quality of services performed meets a high level of professionalism.

Competence also acknowledges the limitations of a CPA's capabilities by suggesting that a consultation or referral may be required when an engagement exceeds the personal competence of a CPA or their firm. Every CPA is responsible for assessing their own competence by evaluating whether their education, experience, and judgment are adequate for the responsibility to be assumed.

There are no specific rules to help a CPA decide if they are competent to perform certain services; it depends on the individual facts and circumstances. In order to make this decision, a CPA in public practice should do the following:

1. Practice in firms that have internal quality control procedures in place to ensure services are competently delivered and adequately supervised.
2. Determine, in their individual judgments, whether the scope and nature of other services provided to a client would create a conflict of interest in the performance of the services for that client.
3. Assess, in their individual judgment, whether an activity is consistent with their role as professionals.

What Would You Do 5-5 presents a fairly common problem encountered by CPA's.

WHAT WOULD YOU DO 5-5
Helping a Friend

You just passed the CPA exam and are working for a public accounting firm when your best friend, Joan, sends you an email asking for help. Joan and her husband have found a great business opportunity and have obtained the last three years' tax returns, lease information and financial statements for the business. They have already decided that this is a terrific opportunity, and, since you have known each other since childhood, they don't trust other professionals as much as they do you. They really want your advice as to whether it is a good idea to buy and if the price is right.

You have never done anything like this, but, as you look at the statements, this business opportunity really does look like a steal. How would you advise Joan?

Chart 5-6

SCOPE AND NATURE OF SERVICES

A member in public practice should observe the Principles of the Code of Professional Conduct in determining the scope and nature of services to be provided. (AICPA Code of Professional Conduct §300.060.01)

CPAs must also be diligent when dealing with clients, employers, and the public. **Diligence** is the responsibility to render services promptly and carefully, to be thorough, and to observe applicable technical and ethical standards. It also requires a CPA to adequately plan and supervise all professional activities for which they are responsible, as can be seen in What Would You Do 5-6.

WHAT WOULD YOU DO 5-6

Your Uncle (Part 1)

For as long as you can remember, you have looked up to your uncle, a CPA who owns his firm and has two bookkeepers as employees. Now that you are graduating from college, he has asked you to work with him and you pay a visit to his office for the first time. In looking around, you see piles of papers and ask him how he knows everything is done correctly and on time; he says that the firm quality control is his experience and he has no time for formal documentation. In addition, his employees have been with him "forever," and he trusts their work completely.

If you were your uncle's client and heard this, how would you react to this? And, now that you are aware of the lack of procedures, what factors should you consider if you want to work for him?

Rules of Professional Conduct: Public Accounting

Based on the general standards, the specific rules for CPAs in public practice are as follows:[3]

---

3. An up-to-date, searchable version of these rules can be found at https://pub.aicpa.org/codeofconduct/Ethics.aspx#.

- Integrity and Objectivity (Chart 5-7)
- Independence (Chart 5-8)
- General Standards (Chart 5-9)
- Acts Discreditable (Chart 5-10)
- Fees and Other Types of Renumeration
- Advertising and Other Forms of Solicitation (Chart 5-11)
- Confidential Information (Chart 5-12)
- Form of Organization and Name Rule (Chart 5-13)

Chart 5-7

INTEGRITY AND OBJECTIVITY

In the performance of any professional service, a member shall maintain objectivity and integrity, shall be free of conflicts of interest, and shall not knowingly misrepresent facts or subordinate his or her judgment to others. (AICPA Code of Professional Conduct §1.100.001)

Integrity is being honest and having strong moral principles; being **objective** means not being influenced by personal feelings, opinions or gain in considering facts. There are many ways a CPA in public practice may face challenges in this area.

A **conflict of interest** can arise in a variety of situations, such as:

- if a public accounting firm has obtained confidential information during the course of the audit, providing services to another client who is planning on acquiring the one that was audited;
- advising two clients at the same time who are competing to acquire the same company when the advice might be relevant to each of their separate competitive positions;
- providing services about the same transaction to both a vendor and a purchaser who are clients of the firm;
- preparing asset valuations for two clients who are in some sort of an adversarial position regarding the same assets;
- representing two clients at the same time, about the same matter, who are in a legal dispute with each other, such as a divorce or the dissolution of a partnership;

- providing a royalty report while at the same time advising the licensee of the correctness of the amounts actually owed;
- advising a client to invest in a business in which the CPA's immediate family member has a financial interest;
- providing strategic advice to a client on its competitive position while having ownership in or similar interest with a competitor of the client;
- advising a client on the acquisition of a business the firm is also interested in acquiring;
- advising a client on the purchase of a product or service while having a royalty or commission agreement with one of the potential vendors of that product or service;
- providing forensic accounting services to a client to evaluate or support possible litigation against another client of the firm;
- providing tax or personal financial planning services for several members of a family whom you know or suspect have opposing interests;
- referring a personal financial planning or tax client to an insurance broker or other service provider under an exclusive arrangement where they also refer clients to the firm;
- providing tax or personal financial planning services to a client's executives, with the advice possibly resulting in recommending to the executive actions that may be adverse to the company;
- serving as a director or an officer of a local United Way or similar organization from which local charities receive funds, some of those charities being clients of the CPA's firm; and
- serving as an officer, director, or shareholder of an entity, and that entity has a loan to or from a client of the firm.

What Would You Do 5-7 illustrates a situation where there may be a conflict of interest.

WHAT WOULD YOU DO 5-7

The IRS Audit

Your construction client is in the midst of a field audit by the IRS. As the audit is concluding, it is pretty obvious it will result in a "no change."

Towards the end of the audit, the agent asks if you can do him a favor. His brother is in the construction industry and pays all of his employees as independent contractors rather than treating them as employees. Since he saw what a great job you did with the business under audit, the agent asks if you can take his brother on as a client.

How would you react to this? What would you consider when making your decision?

Chart 5-8

INDEPENDENCE

A member in public practice shall be independent in the performance of professional services as required by standards promulgated by bodies designated by Council. (AICPA Code of Professional Conduct §1.200.001)

Being **independent** is when a CPA is not influenced or controlled by other people, but, rather, free to make their own decisions. Another way to look at this is being unbiased when making decisions or giving advice.

Being independent in *appearance*, as well as in *fact*, is critical. Note that many conflict of interest situations in the previous list might not result in a conflict of interest, but the mere appearance might cause another to question if the CPA is making an unbiased decision.

There are different rules for independence depending on the CPA's responsibilities:

1. Members of engagement teams cannot have a direct or a material indirect investment in an audit client. In addition, they cannot be a trustee or an executor of an estate that invests directly in an audit client. With some

limited exceptions, they also cannot have loans to or from an audit client. All other professional employees of the firm and their immediate family members cannot have a direct investment of 5% or more in an audit client nor be in a key position with an audit client.

2. If a member of the CPA's immediate family (spouse or equivalent and dependents) is involved with a client, this person cannot be employed in a "key position" with an audit client or it impairs their independence. Other close relatives (parents, brothers and sisters) cannot hold a key position with an audit client, hold a material financial interest or have significant influence over an audit client.

Independence can also be impaired whenever the existence of threat of litigation is present, such as if the CPA is suing for unpaid fees or the client is suing the CPA for malpractice. If the lawsuit causes an adversary position between the client and the CPA, independence would be lost.

Not all services are audits or reviews; non-attest services include accounting, tax, and consulting services. Activities such as financial statement preparation, cash-to-accrual conversions, and reconciliations are considered outside the scope of the attest engagement and, therefore, constitute a non-attest service. Non-attest services specifically addressed in the rules include the following:[4]

- Advisory services
- Appraisal, valuation, or actuarial services
- Benefit plan administration services
- Bookkeeping, payroll, and other disbursement services
- Business risk consulting services
- Corporate finance consulting services
- Executive or employee recruiting services
- Forensic accounting services
- Information systems design, installation, or integration services
- Internal audit services
- Investment advisory or management services
- Tax services

---

4. Association of International Certified Professional Accountants, *AICPA Plain Guide to Independence, August 2017, https://www.aicpa.org/interestareas/professionalethics/resources/tools/downloadabledocuments/plain%20english%20guide.pdf.*

One of the key principles underlying the rules on non-attest services is that the CPA may not assume management responsibilities or even *appear* to assume management responsibilities. Management responsibilities involve leading and directing an entity—including making significant decisions regarding an acquisition—and control of human, financial, physical, and intangible resources. Some examples of activities that would impair independence are as follows:

1. Accepting responsibility to authorize payment of client funds, including signing or cosigning client checks, even only in an emergency situation.
2. In a consulting engagement, acting as a promoter, underwriter or broker-dealer of private placement memoranda or other offering documents.
3. Determining or changing journal entries, accounting codes, classification of transactions or other accounting changes without client approval. For non-public companies, proposing adjusting entries to an attest client's financial statements as part of an audit, review, or compilation is not considered a non-attest service. However, the client must review the entries, understand the effect on its financial statements, and record any adjustments the client believes are appropriate.
4. Preparing source documents or making changes to source documents without client approval.
5. Having custody of client assets or securities.
6. Supervising client personnel in the daily operation of their computer system.
7. Making investment decisions for the client or otherwise having discretionary authority over their investments.
8. Presenting business proposals to a board of directors on behalf of management.

What Would You Do 5-8 demonstrates a potential independence issue.

WHAT WOULD YOU DO 5-8

Board of Directors

A partner in the CPA firm you work for is on the board of directors of a private school. He is now "termed out" and cannot serve on the board anymore, so he asks you to take his place. Not wanting to upset your boss, you agree.

As you settle in and go to board meetings, you see why the partner was so anxious—it really is a nice group of people who are dedicated to their community and education. Other than an attorney, you are the only non-education professional on the board, so they look to you for tax and accounting advice.

At the annual meeting the audit is presented, and you notice the name on the audit report—the firm you work for! There is no audit committee since the treasurer, a history teacher, handled all of the arrangements. You notice the report is comparative, which means that the audit has been handled by your firm for at least two years. When you ask, the treasurer says that the firm has performed the audit for the last ten years, even before the partner joined the board.

What factors should you consider in this situation?

Unpaid fees are basically a loan to the client from the CPA. Since invoicing and collections are a normal part of all business activities, independence is only impaired if fees, billed or unbilled, are for services provided prior to over one year from the date of the financial statement report (§1.500.008).

Chart 5-9

GENERAL STANDARDS

A member shall comply with the following standards and with any interpretations thereof by bodies designated by Council:

a. Professional Competence. Undertake only those professional services that the member or the member's firm can reasonably expect to be completed with professional competence.
b. Due Professional Care. Exercise due professional care in the performance of professional services.
c. Planning and Supervision. Adequately plan and supervise the performance of professional services.
d. Sufficient Relevant Data. Obtain sufficient relevant data to afford a reasonable basis for conclusions or recommendations in relation to any professional services performed. (AICPA Code of Professional Conduct §1.300.001)

Competence means the CPA and the firm possess the appropriate technical qualifications to perform the specific services as well as supervise and evaluate the quality of work performed. Competence includes knowledge of the applicable standards, the techniques and technical subject matter involved, and the ability to exercise sound judgment in applying this knowledge.

When a CPA agrees to perform professional services, it is implied that he or she has the competence to accomplish the job according to professional standards, with reasonable care and diligence. A normal part of providing professional services may involve additional research or consulting with others to gain sufficient competence. If the CPA does not have, or cannot get, sufficient competence, they should engage somebody who does have that experience. What Would You Do 5-9 discusses how this might be handled.

WHAT WOULD YOU DO 5-9

A New Client

After working for a large CPA firm, you are excited to start your own. Since your experience was auditing manufacturing companies, you feel competent in that industry; indeed, your first two clients are manufacturers.

After six months working with one of the clients, an IRS audit letter shows up. Your experience is in accounting/auditing but, as you look at the letter, it looks like all they are asking for are some inventory records and some entertainment receipts. In addition, they want documentation backing up the president's salary.

How would you feel representing the client at the audit? Are there any actions you can take that might help in your representation?

When a CPA exercises **due care**, he or she observes the profession's technical and ethical standards, continually strives to improve competence and the quality of services and discharges professional responsibility to the best of their ability. It also means taking on the responsibility to render services promptly and carefully, to be thorough, and to observe applicable technical and ethical standards.

Due care also requires a CPA to adequately **plan and supervise** whatever professional services they or their firm is responsible for. Keeping in mind What Would You Do 5-6, this can now be looked at in a different light in What Would You Do 5-10.

WHAT WOULD YOU DO 5-10

Your Uncle (Part 2)

Remember your uncle, the one you looked up to in What Would You Do 5-6? Now that you understand what due care requires, how do you feel about his practice? Does this change your mind about working for him?

Finally, no matter what a CPA does—bookkeeping, tax preparation, consulting or attest services, or even using a third-party expert—they must obtain sufficient relevant data to support the work product and comply with all of the applicable technical standards. What Would You Do 5-11 discusses this dilemma.

WHAT WOULD YOU DO 5-11

A New Client

One day a potential new client walks in off the street. He is a young, energetic guy who recently started a service business and is well known in the community; in fact, he was recently named one of the top ten "young entrepreneurs to watch" in the country. You are excited to meet such a famous and potentially lucrative client.

In talking about his business, the potential client indicates that he needs some financial statements but has been too busy running the business to prepare them properly. He asks if you can compile some GAAP-compliant statements and, of course, you answer "yes", so he agrees to bring you some numbers in the morning. When you ask the source of the information he will be bringing he says, "I really don't have books, but I'll bring you what my records show."

Should you take the job? What factors would make it acceptable to take on? What would cause you to decline?

Chart 5-10

ACTS DISCREDITABLE

A member shall not commit an act discreditable to the profession. (AICPA Code of Professional Conduct §1.400.001)

A **discreditable act** is something done that may damage the reputation and integrity of the profession, even those not covered by other rules. Some of these acts are considered unethical:

1. Retention of client records and adjusting entries necessary to complete the client's records.
2. Discrimination and harassment in the workplace.
3. Failure to follow standards, procedures or other requirements in governmental audits.
4. Negligence when preparing financial statements.

5. Failure to follow governmental bodies, commissions or other regulatory agencies rules when performing an audit or similar services.
6. Solicitation or disclosure of CPA examination questions and answers.
7. Failure to file a tax return—including personal, business and employment—and pay taxes.
8. Not following state accountancy laws and board of accountancy rules and regulations regarding the use of the CPA's credential.

As discussed in What Would You Do 5-12, sometimes this is not an easy call.

WHAT WOULD YOU DO 5-12

Bad Deeds

Your friend is a CPA in public practice who is going through a rough patch. Three things happened in the last year that he needs your advice on:

1. He had a DUI (drunk driving) conviction.
2. He is in the midst of an extramarital affair.
3. He stole $5,000 from his employer with the use of a "phantom employee" and does not expect to get caught.

Do you believe any of these are discreditable acts as defined by the AICPA? Why or why not?

There are many ways public CPAs can be paid. **Fees and Other Types of Renumeration** include commissions, contingent fees and referral fees (AICPA Code of Professional Conduct §1.500).

Two types of fee arrangements—contingent fees and commissions—are prohibited for most attest clients, even though the fee is not related to that service. Fees fixed by a court or other public authority and, in tax matters, fees based on the results of judicial proceedings or the findings of governmental agencies are exempt from this rule.

A **contingent fee** is an arrangement where no fee is charged unless a specified result is attained or the amount of the fee depends on the results of the CPA or their firm's services (AICPA Code of Professional Conduct §1.510). Some examples of contingent fees are as follows:

1. Your firm receives a finder's fee for helping a client locate a buyer for some of their assets.
2. You perform a consulting engagement to decrease a client's operating costs and receive a percentage of the money saved.

A **commission** is any compensation paid to a CPA or their firm for recommending or referring a third-party's product or service to a client or recommending or referring a client's product or service to a third party (AICPA Code of Professional Conduct §1.520). Some examples of commissions that, *if disclosed to the client*, are allowed are as follows:

1. You or your firm refers a client to a financial planning firm that pays you a commission for the referral.
2. You or your firm sells accounting software to a client and receives a percentage of the sales price (a commission) from a software company.
3. You or your firm refers a non-client to an insurance company client that pays you a percentage of any premiums received (a commission) from the non-client.

Commissions or contingent fee arrangements with a client are never allowed if a CPA or their firm provides:

1. an audit or review of financial statements;
2. a compilation of financial statements if a third party (for example, a bank or an investor) will rely on the financial statements, and the report does not disclose a lack of independence; and
3. an examination of prospective financial statements.

A CPA may have commission and contingent fee arrangements with those associated with a client, such as officers, directors, and principal shareholders, or with an employee benefit plan that is sponsored by a client (when the plan itself is not an audit client). For example, you may receive a commission from a non-client insurer if you refer an officer of an attest client to the insurer and the officer purchases a policy. Even though this situation is permitted, you are still required to tell the officer, in writing, that you received a commission for making the referral.

Finally, payments by a CPA to obtain a client are allowed as long as disclosure is made to the client.

Chart 5-11

ADVERTISING AND OTHER TYPES OF SOLICITATION

A member in public practice shall not seek to obtain clients by advertising or other forms of solicitation in a manner that is false, misleading, or deceptive. Solicitation by the use of coercion, over-reaching, or harassing conduct is prohibited. (AICPA Code of Professional Conduct §1.600.001)

The rules on **advertising and solicitation** are there to prevent CPAs from false or deceptive advertising. It does not prohibit advertising that includes testimonials or endorsements.

Some examples of promotional efforts considered false, misleading, or deceptive are those that:

1. create false or unjustified expectations of favorable results;
2. imply the ability to influence any court, tribunal, regulatory agency, or similar body or official;
3. contain a representation that the CPA will perform specific professional services in current or future periods for a stated fee, estimated fee, or fee range when it was likely at the time of the representation that such fees would be substantially increased and the prospective client was not informed of that likelihood; and
4. contain any other representations that would be likely to cause a reasonable person to misunderstand or be deceived.

Much of today's advertising is done via social media; What Would You Do 5-13 discusses how one must be wary when designing the promotion.

WHAT WOULD YOU DO 5-13

Social Media

You are thinking of how to get clients for your accounting firm and decide that social media is the way to do it. In contemplating using LinkedIn, Facebook and Twitter, among others, how can you avoid the following potential ethical violations?

1. False or misleading statements
2. Disclosure of confidential information
3. Creating an attorney-client relationship with potential clients

---

Chart 5-12

CONFIDENTIAL INFORMATION

A member in public practice shall not disclose any confidential client information without the specific consent of the client. (AICPA Code of Professional Conduct §1.700.001)

A fundamental expectation that clients have of a CPA in public practice is that all all information about a client's business affairs remains confidential to the full extent possible. Maintaining strict **confidentiality** is critical in establishing mutual trust.

A CPA must obtain the specific consent of the client, generally in writing, before disclosing client information. There are four exceptions to this rule:

1. Complying with a valid subpoena, summons, or applicable statutes and government regulations
2. Conducting a review of a CPA's professional practice under AICPA or state CPA authority
3. Initiating or responding to a complaint made by a professional ethics organization
4. A review of client confidential information in connection with the purchase, sale, or merger of a practice

In many industries a nondisclosure agreement is required from all vendors. What Would You Do 5-14 addresses this issue.

WHAT WOULD YOU DO 5-14

The Nondisclosure Agreement

Your firm landed a great audit client, an up-and-coming tech company with inventions they think will change the world while making a lot of money for the owners. When they return your engagement letter, they enclose a "non-disclosure agreement" that contains, among other things, these three clauses:

1. An "as is" clause that prohibits your firm from relying on client information.
2. A return/destruction of information clause requiring you to promptly return all client confidential information or, on completion of the audit and upon their request, destroy it.
3. A clause prohibiting disclosure to third parties.

How would you respond to each of these items, balancing professional standards with the client's need to ensure the safety of their intellectual property?

Note that *confidentiality* is very different from the legal concept of **privileged communication**. Federal and most state laws allow for attorney/client, doctor/ patient and priest/parishioner privileged communications, meaning what they discuss can never be revealed unless the client allows it. Federal and state statutes for CPAs are much narrower; some states do not even have privileged communication for CPAs. What Would You Do 5-15 addresses the issue of confidentiality.

WHAT WOULD YOU DO 5-15

Client Receivables

You are compiling the financial statements for a telephone repair company and notice an account receivable from another of your clients that is past due sixty days. You are pretty sure the other client did not accrue the account payable on their books.

Would it be ethical to look at the other client's books and see if was accrued? If you did look and it was not reflected on their books, what would you do?

> ## Chart 5-13
> ## FORM OF ORGANIZATION AND NAME
>
> A member may practice public accounting only in a form of organization permitted by law or regulation whose characteristics conform to resolutions of Council. A member shall not practice public accounting under a firm name that is misleading. Names of one or more past owners may be included in the firm name of a successor organization. A firm may not designate itself as "Members of the American Institute of Certified Public Accountants" unless all its CPA owners are members of the AICPA. (AICPA Code of Professional Conduct §1.800.001)

Any **form of organization** allowed by state law is allowed, as long as it conforms to the AICPA regulations. CPAs must own a majority of the financial interests in a firm that provides attest services to the public. This means that CPAs are responsible, financially and otherwise, for their attest work.

Non-CPA owners can have a partial ownership interest in a firm if they, for example, provide tax or advisory services. In addition, not only the AICPA but most state boards of accountancy do not allow a false, misleading or deceptive name, including one that might imply the ability to provide services not justified. This is illustrated in What Would You Do 5-16.

> ## WHAT WOULD YOU DO 5-16
> ### Your New Tax Practice
>
> You are excited to begin as a tax professional in your community and have lots of potential clients. In setting up your office, you decide on an LLC structure; as part of this you have to register a name with the state. Your brother is in marketing and comes up with two great names—Maximum Tax Refunds LLC and Maximum Tax Deductions LLC. You like the name No Tax Audits LLC.
>
> Which, if any, of these names are acceptable under the AICPA rules? Propose three alternative names that might be allowed but still be unique and good for marketing your services.

Rules of Professional Conduct: Private Accounting

Not all CPAs are in public accounting; CPAs can work in private industry, government and teaching positions, as well as be retired or unemployed. While many of the standards are similar to CPAs in public practice, there are differences as well. The pertinent standards for CPAs in private industry are:[5]

- integrity and objectivity (Chart 5-14);
- general standards (Chart 5-15); and
- acts discreditable (Chart 5-16).

Chart 5-14

INTEGRITY AND OBJECTIVITY

In the performance of any professional service, a member shall maintain objectivity and integrity, shall be free of conflicts of interest, and shall not knowingly misrepresent facts or subordinate his or her judgment to others. (AICPA Code of Professional Conduct §2.100.001)

A **conflict of interest** will create a situation where the CPA must consider their **integrity and objectivity**. This can happen when the CPA takes on a job involving those whose interests are in conflict or the CPA's interests and the other party are in conflict. Some examples of situations that may occur in private accounting are:

a. serving in a management or board position and acquiring confidential information from one organization that could be used to the advantage or disadvantage of the other organization;
b. helping both parties who are dissolving a marriage or partnership;
c. preparing financial information for members of management who are contemplating a management buy-out;
d. being responsible for selecting a vendor for your employer when you or your immediate family member could benefit financially from the transaction; and

---

5. An up-to-date, searchable version of these rules can be found at https://pub.aicpa.org/codeofconduct/Ethics.aspx#.

e. serving in a governance capacity or influencing an organization that is approving investments for the company in which one of those investments will increase the value of you or your immediate family members' personal investments.

Sometimes there may be **pressure exerted** to "look the other way." Some examples of this are:

- pressure from a family member bidding to become a vendor to select the family member over another prospective vendor;
- pressure to report misleading financial results to meet investor, analyst, or lender expectations;
- pressure from elected officials to misrepresent programs or projects to voters;
- pressure from management to misstate income, expense, or rates of return to influence capital projects and acquisitions;
- pressure from superiors to approve or process costs that are not legitimate business expenses;
- pressure to suppress internal audit reports that have adverse findings;
- pressure to do something without sufficient competence or due care;
- pressure from superiors to inappropriately take shortcuts on your work product;
- pressure from superiors to perform a task without sufficient skills or training or with unrealistic deadlines;
- pressure to manipulate performance indicators for those who may gain from a compensation or incentive program;
- pressure from others, either inside or outside of your organization, to offer gifts or entertainment to inappropriately influence your judgment or decision-making process; and
- pressure from colleagues to accept inappropriate gifts or entertainment from potential vendors in a bidding process.

What Would You Do 5-17 looks at an example of how a situation might be handled in two scenarios.

WHAT WOULD YOU DO 5-17

No Receipts

Jose works as an auditor for the State of Texas and has been assigned to the audit of a large school district. The following conversation takes place about a travel voucher that was reimbursed:

Employee: I've requested the documentation you asked for, but the hotel says it's no longer in their system.

Jose: Don't you have the credit card receipt or credit card statement?

Employee: I paid cash.

Jose: What about a copy of the hotel bill?

Employee: I threw it out.

Jose: That's a problem. We have to document all your travel expenses for the city manager's office.

Employee: I can't produce documents that the hotel can't find. What do you want me to do?

What should Jose do in this situation? How might your answer change if the city manager had signed off on the expense reimbursement when it was initially submitted?

Chart 5-15

GENERAL STANDARDS

A member shall comply with the following standards and with any interpretations thereof by bodies designated by Council.

a. Professional Competence. Undertake only those professional services that the member or the member's firm can reasonably expect to be completed with professional competence.

b. Due Professional Care. Exercise due professional care in the performance of professional services.

c. Planning and Supervision. Adequately plan and supervise the performance of professional services.

d. Sufficient Relevant Data. Obtain sufficient relevant data to afford a reasonable basis for conclusions or recommendations in relation to any professional services performed. (AICPA Code of Professional Conduct §2.300.001)

Professional Competence means the CPA has the technical qualifications to perform professional services and supervises and evaluates the quality of work performed. This includes not only knowledge of the profession's standards and the technical subject matter involved but also the ability to exercise sound judgment in applying these skills. Similar to public accounting, it requires that the CPA comply with professional standards. This can be even be applied prior to obtaining a job, as illustrated in What Would You Do 5-18.

WHAT WOULD YOU DO 5-18

A New Job

You have been made an offer to work at the public college you attended six years ago. Even though you are happy at the CPA firm you are currently with, the long hours have taken a toll, and you would love to get the public employee benefits package. Not to mention, you love the title "Vice President of Administration."

One problem: you never worked in a governmental job nor did a budget based on fund accounting. On the upside, you have been told there is a budget analyst who will work under you.

What factors should you consider in deciding to accept or reject the job? Would you take it? Why?

Chart 5-16

ACTS DISCREDITABLE

A member shall not commit an act discreditable to the profession. (AICPA Code of Professional Conduct §2.400.001)

While on the surface this rule sounds exactly like the standard for public CPAs (Chart 5-10), the standard for private CPAs is a bit different. In this area, **discreditable acts** encompass the following:

- Discrimination and harassment in employment practices.
- Solicitation or disclosure of CPA examination questions and answers.

- Failure to file a tax return or pay a tax liability. This includes not only the CPA's taxes, but also the timely payment payroll and other taxes collected on behalf of others, such as the employer.
- Negligence in the preparation of financial statements or maintaining records.
- Disregard of governmental bodies, commissions, or other regulatory agency rules. There are many governmental agencies, such as the SEC, Federal Communications Commission and state insurance commissions. A material departure from their requirements is a violation of this rule unless the CPA discloses in the financial statements or related information that such requirements were not followed and the applicable reasons.
- Confidential information obtained from employment or volunteer activities. While this should be obvious, there is always a possibility of inadvertent disclosure, particularly to a close business associate or close relative or immediate family member. When changing jobs, a CPA should not use confidential employer information to their personal advantage or the advantage of a current (or prospective) employer. The requirement of confidentiality continues even after the job is over.

Some examples of situations in which a CPA is permitted, or may be required, to disclose confidential information or it may be appropriate to do so are when:

- disclosure is permitted by law and authorized by the employer;
- disclosure is required by law; for example, to comply with a validly issued and enforceable subpoena or summons or inform the appropriate public authorities of violations of law that have been discovered;
- initiating a complaint with, or responding to any inquiry made by, the AICPA or an investigative or disciplinary body of a state CPA society, board of accountancy, or other regulatory body;
- protecting your professional interests in legal proceedings;
- complying with professional standards and other ethics requirements;
- reporting potential concerns regarding questionable accounting, auditing, or other matters to the employer's confidential complaint hotline or other areas in the organization who are charged with governance; and
- obtaining financing with lenders, communicate with vendors, clients, and customers, the external accountant, attorneys, regulators, and other business professionals on behalf of your employer.

Sometimes there is an inadvertent slip of confidential information, as shown in What Would You Do 5-19.

WHAT WOULD YOU DO 5-19
On the Train

You are the treasurer and a member of the board of directors of a non-profit that is considering a merger with another exempt organization. You are on the way back from a business meeting and notice there is another person two rows away talking loudly into their phone. Just about everybody on the train can hear his conversation.

When you overhear a name mentioned, your ears perk up—the loud talker is the chief negotiator for the organization you are negotiating with! You have never met this man, but it is very clear who he is. He appears to be talking with other members and planning strategy. You believe that the loud talker is also a CPA.

What ethical standards have been violated? Is it ethical for you to use the information you are overhearing?

PCAOB Rules for Auditors

The **Public Company Accounting Oversight Board** (PCAOB) has specific rules for auditors of publicly held companies. Some of the general rules parallel the AICPA professional standards and amplify them. Three of these general rules are:[6]

- independence;
- training and proficiency; and
- due professional care.

An **independence** in mental attitude is expected to be maintained by the auditor or auditors of publicly held companies (§AS 1005). This requires that the auditor be without bias with respect to the client; otherwise, the auditor would not be impartial, no matter how technically proficient the auditor is. There is an obligation for fairness not only to management and owners of a business but also

---

6. An up-to-date, searchable version of these rules can be found at https://pcaobus.org/Standards/Auditing.

to creditors and those who might otherwise rely (at least in part) on the independent auditor's report.

The PCAOB recognizes that the AICPA has rules to guard against the loss of independence. The PCAOB goes a bit further, noting that independence is a matter of personal quality rather than of rules and objective tests.

An auditor must have adequate **training and proficiency** (§AS 1010). This means that an audit is to be performed by a person (or persons) having adequate technical training and proficiency as an auditor. No matter how capable a person may be in other fields, including business and finance, one cannot meet the requirements of the auditing standards without proper education and experience in the field of auditing.

This training must emphasize technical areas and include a number of general education courses as well. An inexperienced assistant must obtain professional experience with the proper supervision and review of their work by a more experienced superior. The nature and extent of supervision and review would, of course, reflect wide variances in the industries and work performed. The engagement partner must exercise seasoned judgment in their supervision and review of the work done and judgments exercised by his subordinates.

Training of a professional includes a continual awareness of developments taking place in business and in the profession. It includes studying, understanding applying new pronouncements on accounting principles and auditing procedures as they are.

An auditor must exercise **due professional care** (§AS 1015) in the planning and performance of the audit, as well as the preparation of the report.

Due professional care looks at what the independent auditor does and how well he or she does it. As discussed in this standard, an auditor should possess "the degree of skill commonly possessed" by other auditors and should exercise it with "reasonable care and diligence" (that is, with due professional care). Auditors should be assigned to tasks and supervised commensurate with their level of knowledge, skill, and ability so that they can evaluate the audit evidence they are examining. The engagement partner should know, at a minimum, the relevant professional accounting and auditing standards and should be knowledgeable about the client. That partner is responsible for the assignment of tasks to, and supervision of, the members of the engagement team.

Due professional care requires the auditor to exercise **professional skepticism**, which is an attitude that includes a questioning mind and a critical assessment of audit evidence. The auditor uses their knowledge, skill, and ability to diligently perform, in good faith and with integrity, the gathering and objective evaluation of evidence.

Gathering and objectively evaluating audit evidence requires the auditor to consider the competency and sufficiency of the evidence. Since evidence is gathered and evaluated throughout the audit, professional skepticism should be exercised throughout the audit process. The auditor neither assumes that management is dishonest nor assumes unquestioned honesty. In exercising professional skepticism, the auditor should not be satisfied with less than persuasive evidence because of a belief that management is honest.

The exercise of due professional care allows the auditor to obtain **reasonable assurance** about whether the financial statements are free of material misstatement, whether caused by error or fraud, or whether any material weaknesses exist as of the date of management's assessment.

The auditor's objective is to obtain sufficient appropriate evidential matter to provide them with a reasonable basis for forming an opinion. Even with good faith and integrity, mistakes and errors in judgment can be made. In the majority of cases, the auditor has to rely on evidence that is persuasive rather than convincing.

Sometimes an auditor is put in an uncomfortable situation, as discussed in What Would You Do 5-20.

WHAT WOULD YOU DO 5-20

No Supervision

Soon after finishing college, you land a great job and are one of two professionals performing an audit of a small, publicly held company. You are impressed that just you and the senior are staffed on such an important client.

You both show up first thing on Monday and get set up in the client's conference room. The senior introduces you to the client and you take a walk around the plant to get oriented. At about 10:00 a.m., the senior gets an email from the partner that another client is planning a public offering later that week and her services are needed immediately in the office. The senior tells you to take a look at the prior year's working papers, write a program and start the audit. When you give her a quizzical look she says, "That is how I learned. Just follow last year, and if you need anything, email me."

Does this comply with the PCAOB standards? How would you handle this situation?

Enforcement

Many states have **enforcement** statutes that are similar to the AICPA Code of Professional Conduct. Generally, a violation of these rules is reported to the state board of accountancy, investigated and, if necessary, enforced. Depending on the state, sanctions can range from requiring a set number of continuing professional education hours or classes to suspension or even revocation of the CPA license. In some situations, criminal charges can be filed.[7]

The PCAOB has authority over auditors of public companies. This includes the professionals who are providing the auditing and non-attest services. Through the SEC, they have the authority to levy fines against accounting firms, prohibit the firms and the professionals from auditing public companies, as well as refer cases to the US attorney for criminal prosecution.

Case 5-1

ERNST & YOUNG[8]

The public accounting firm Ernst & Young agreed to pay $9.3 million to settle charges that two of the firm's audit partners got too close to their clients on a personal level and violated rules that ensure firms maintain their objectivity and impartiality during audits.

The SEC investigations found that the senior partner on an engagement team for the audit of a New York-based public company maintained an improperly close friendship with its chief financial officer, and a different partner serving on an engagement team for the audit of another public company was romantically involved with its chief accounting officer. Ernst & Young misrepresented in audit reports issued with the companies' financial statements that it maintained its independence throughout these audits. These were the first SEC enforcement actions where an accounting firm did not do enough to detect or prevent these partners from getting too close to their clients and compromising their roles as independent auditors.

---

7. For a discussion of the specific rules in California, refer to Chapter 7.

8. US Securities and Exchange Commission, "Ernst & Young, Former Partners Charged with Violating Auditor Independence Rules," *SEC.gov,* September 19, 2016, *https://www.sec. gov/news/pressrelease/2016-187.html. Also, SEC Accounting and Auditing Enforcement Release No. 3802 File No. 3-17552 and Release No. 3803 File No. 3-17553.*

In one case, some of the other partners became aware of excessive entertainment spending but took no action to confirm that the partner was complying with his independence obligations. Without admitting guilt, the firm agreed to pay $4.975 million in sanctions; the partner paid a $45,000 penalty and was suspended from appearing and practicing before the SEC.

In the second case, an auditor had a romantic relationship with a financial executive while she served on the engagement team auditing his company. Her supervisor was aware of facts suggesting the improper relationship yet failed to perform a reasonable inquiry or raise concerns. Without admitting guilt, the firm agreed to pay $4.366 million in sanctions, two of the CPAs working on the engagement paid penalties of $25,000 each and were suspended from appearing and practicing before the SEC.

A member of the AICPA can only be charged with a violation of the Code of Professional Conduct. The AICPA has agreements with some state boards of accountancy to share information, and vice versa. In addition, many of the state boards require CPAs to report disciplinary actions that may result in enforcement.

The AICPA developed a **Joint Ethics Enforcement Program** with the state CPA societies. This allows complaints against an AICPA member to be filed either with the AICPA or the state society. If the member is found to have violated standards, they can be admonished, suspended for up to two years or expelled from the AICPA. If the violation is a departure from technical standards, additional requirements—such as continuing professional education—can also be assigned.

There are also **automatic disciplinary provisions** under the AICPA bylaws that call for suspension or termination of the membership without a hearing in these situations:[9]

1. A crime punishable by imprisonment for more than one year.
2. Willful failure to file any income tax return that the member, as an individual taxpayer, is required by law to file.
3. The filing of a false or fraudulent income tax return on the member's or a client's behalf.

---

9. AICPA Bylaws §7.3.1. The full text of the bylaws can be found at https://www.aicpa.org/about/governance/bylaws.html

4. Willful aiding in the preparation and presentation of a false and fraudulent income tax return of a client.

5. The member's CPA certificate is revoked, withdrawn or canceled as a disciplinary measure by any governmental agency, including, with certain exceptions, failure to meet continuing professional education requirements.

Discussion Questions

1. In your own words, explain the importance of each of the six principles in the Code.

2. To whom, and in what circumstances, does the Code of Professional Conduct apply?

3. Do you believe that independence is impaired when an auditor is hired, paid and can be fired by the company that they are auditing? Can you think of a better way?

4. Would advising an audit client on how to structure a business transaction to achieve specific accounting treatment under GAAP be a threat to independence? Why?

5. What problems do you see when an auditor relies extensively on management's representations on the financial statements?

6. What individuals are considered "immediate family members," and what activities could impair a CPA's independence? How about "close relatives" and "other professional employees"?

7. Do you believe that a CPA should be able to advertise? What guidelines would you recommend? Are there any areas you believe should be avoided?

8. When could a partner or other professional employee of a CPA firm accept a job with a client of a firm?

9. Describe, in your own words, the AICPA ethical standards that apply to a CPA who is also the CFO of a company.

10. Under what circumstances can a CPA ethically disclose confidential client information?

11. What forms of organization are permitted under AICPA standards?

12. Specifically, how are PCAOB rules different from AICPA standards?

13. What is the role of the various state boards of accountancy in ethical matters? What rules do they use to evaluate possible ethical violations? What potential punishment is available to them?

14. If you were an auditor, would you but a new car at a dealership you are currently auditing for 15% off the list price? Why do you feel this way?

15. If you were a management accountant, would you buy a product from a supplier for personal use at 20% off of list price?

16. A client is indebted to a CPA for unpaid fees and has offered to sign unsecured interest-bearing notes. Would acceptance of these notes have any bearing on the CPA's independence with the client? Why?

17. Your audit client's bookkeeper resigned three months ago, and the books are not up-to-date. The board of directors meeting is fast approaching, so the client asks your firm, as the outside auditors, for help. They specifically ask for Margaret Jones, who worked on the audit, to help since she is familiar with their system and can be efficient with little training. What are the ethical issues you would have to consider in this situation?

18. You decide to leave the CPA firm you have worked at for the last five years. Can you post some negative comments about your former employer on your personal Twitter account? Can you email or call the clients you worked with at the firm to let them know you are leaving? Can you take copies of their financial statements when you go?

19. Your firm provides bookkeeping and other non-attest services for a variety of clients. During lunch at a meeting of accounting professionals, you overhear that many of them are sending the work to offshore centers in countries like

India and the Philippines where the wages are about half of what are paid in the United States. This sounds appealing; what ethical issues should be taken into account when considering such a move?

20. You are the senior CPA at a multi-office CPA firm, assigned to the audit of a privately held business and a major client of the firm. During the audit, you find a material error that causes the company's income to be significantly misstated. You know that accounting standards clearly state that any potential material adjustment must be documented in the workpapers and the final determination of materiality is then made by the partner in charge of the audit. Before wrapping up the field work, the audit manager asks you not to mention this adjustment in the workpapers. He says that, since the business is closely held and there are no tax implications, the partner has decided not to inform them about the adjustment. How would you handle this situation?

Case Study[10]

Scott London was a senior partner at KPMG in charge of the audit practice for clients in California, Arizona and Nevada. He also personally oversaw audits of Herbalife and Skechers. He worked at KPMG for thirty years. Over a two-year period, he passed information on several companies by reading his friend, Brian Shaw, news releases before they were issued, telling him about planned acquisitions and giving him advance word about earnings that were not yet public. That allowed Shaw to make many profitable trades.

For example, Shaw purchased thousands of Herbalife shares in the weeks before an announcement of the company's record sales. The announcement sent Herbalife shares up 13%, and Shaw made a profit of about $450,000. Shaw was also told that another KPMG client, Pacific Capital Bancorp, was about to be acquired by Union Bank. Pacific Capital's shares increased 57% when the news was announced and Shaw made $365,000.

Regulators became suspicious of Shaw's well-timed trades and began an investigation. The regulators had Shaw secretly record conversations with London and was filmed by the FBI handing London an envelope of cash. Shaw pleaded guilty to conspiracy to commit insider trading.

---

10. Securities and Exchange Commission v. Scott London and Bryan Shaw, April 11, 2013, United States District Court, Central District of California, Case CV 13-02558.

KPMG fired London and withdrew several audits of Herbalife and footwear maker Skechers, plus resigned as the auditor of both clients. A criminal case was filed a few days later.

At the trial, London said he was helping a friend whose jewelry business was in financial trouble, thinking regulators would not look at the "small fish." London believed Shaw made about $200,000 on the trades when, in fact, it was over $1.2 million. He also admitted to receiving $60,000 in cash and a $12,000 Rolex watch, part of which was on the FBI film. Compared to the earnings he made as a very senior audit partner in a major accounting firm, this was insignificant.

London was sentenced to fourteen months in prison (it could have been up to twenty years) and charged with civil penalties—not to mention the legal fees and damage to his reputation.

Case Study Questions

1. Do you believe that it was necessary for KPMG to retract their opinion on the audits London was in charge of? How about resign as the auditor?

2. Name three ways accounting firms can be sure that their partners and employees do not release confidential information.

CHAPTER 6

TAX ETHICS

The income tax created more criminals than any other single act of government.

—Barry Goldwater, US Senator from Arizona (1909–1998)

While most CPAs begin in auditing, management or other related fields, at some point many will provide tax services for clients. This chapter discusses ethics in tax areas such as compliance, planning and tax shelters. There are two sources of ethics guidance in the tax area:

- Statements on Standards for Tax Services
- Internal Revenue Service Circular 230

Statements on Standards for Tax Services

Statements on Standards for Tax Services (SSTS) are issued by the AICPA. They explain a CPA's responsibility to their clients and to the tax system. The standards are as follows:[1]

---

1. Association of International Certified Professional Accountants, "Statements on Standards for Tax Services," accessed June 26, 2018, https://www.aicpa.org/interestareas/tax/resources/standardsethics/statementsonstandardsfortaxservices.html.

- Tax Return Positions (Chart 6-1)
- Answers to Questions on Returns (Chart 6-2)
- Certain Procedural Aspects of Preparing Returns (Chart 6-3)
- Use of Estimates (Chart 6-4)
- Departure from a Position Previously Concluded in an Administrative Proceeding or Court Decision (Chart 6-5)
- Knowledge of Error: Return Preparation and Administrative Proceedings (Chart 6-6)
- Form and Content of Advice to Taxpayers (Chart 6-7)

As seen in Chart 6-1, AICPA Statements on Standards for Tax Services 1 addresses a CPA's obligation to inform a client of tax disclosure responsibilities and potential penalties. Note that informing a client is not only an AICPA requirement but is also required by the IRS and many state and local authorities. What Would You Do 6-1 presents an unusual application of these rules.

Chart 6-1

TAX RETURN POSITIONS

A member should determine and comply with the standards, if any, imposed by the applicable taxing authority with respect to recommending a tax return position or preparing or signing a tax return.

If the applicable taxing authority has no written standards with respect to recommending a tax return position or preparing or signing a tax return, or if its standards are lower than the standards set forth in this paragraph, the following standards will apply:

a. A member should not recommend a tax return position or prepare or sign a tax return taking a position unless the member has a good-faith belief that the position has at least a realistic possibility of being sustained administratively or judicially on its merits if challenged.

b. Notwithstanding the above, a member may recommend a tax return position if the member (i) concludes that there is a reasonable basis for the position and (ii) advises the taxpayer to appropriately disclose that position. Notwithstanding paragraph 5(a), a member may prepare or sign a tax return that reflects a position if (i) the member concludes there is a reasonable basis for the position and (ii) the position is appropriately disclosed.

When recommending a tax return position or when preparing or signing a tax return on which a position is taken, a member should, when relevant, advise the taxpayer regarding potential penalty consequences of such tax return position and the opportunity, if any, to avoid such penalties through disclosure.

A member should not recommend a tax return position or prepare or sign a tax return reflecting a position that the member knows exploits the audit selection process of a taxing authority or serves as a mere arguing position advanced solely to obtain leverage in a negotiation with a taxing authority.

When recommending a tax return position, a member has both the right and the responsibility to be an advocate for the taxpayer with respect to any position satisfying the aforementioned standards. (AICPA Statements on Standards for Tax Services 1)

WHAT WOULD YOU DO 6-1

Overstating Income

Sofia, one of your long-standing clients comes to you with an unusual request—she wants to add $40,000 to her business' gross receipts, even though there will be more income and self-employment taxes. This seems a bit odd, since most of your clients want to pay as little tax as possible, not more.

Sofia explains that she owns some rental properties and is always looking for more. Since the bank asks for copies of her tax returns as proof of income and to determine if she can repay the loans, by adding $40,000 to her income, she will more easily qualify for either new loans or refinancing. She believes that this is a form of "cheap insurance" and does not mind paying the additional tax.

There are penalties in the tax law for understating your income, but none that you know of for purposely overstating it. What would you do in this situation?

A CPA is often asked how to report a transaction or amounts that will be on a client's tax return. Perhaps surprisingly, many routine items in return preparation and tax are actually considered tax return positions under this rule. Examples include:

- the choice of a depreciation or accounting method;
- Section 179 depreciation and the bonus depreciation;
- installment reporting of gains;
- reporting business mileage;
- business travel costs; and
- payroll tax return preparation items and amounts.

A CPA has an obligation to advise their client of relevant tax return disclosure responsibilities and potential penalties prior to recommending a tax return position or preparing or signing the tax return. But what if there are no written standards or clear law?

Under Interpretation 101-1, the position should not be recommended unless the CPA has a good-faith belief that the recommendation has at least a **realistic possibility of success** if it is challenged by the taxing authorities. Alternatively, the CPA can recommend a tax position if there is a **reasonable basis** for that position and they advise the client to disclose the position.

This interpretation specifically does not allow a CPA to play the "audit lottery game" or advance a position that is just a ploy in a negotiation with the taxing authority. As illustrated in What Would You Do 6-2, a CPA cannot recommend an overly aggressive position to a client in the hope that the IRS or other taxing authority does not audit the return.

WHAT WOULD YOU DO 6-2

Enjoying the Family

One of your more successful clients, a dentist, brings you his tax information and you are surprised to see that he has over $45,000 of travel costs. When you ask him about this, he indicates that he goes to dental conferences in various places around the world, stays in very nice hotels, eats very nice meals and has documentation to support all this. It still seems like a lot, so when you ask to see some of the receipts, you notice that the first-class airfare not only has his name, but also the names of his wife, two children and mother-in-law. As you give him a funny look your client says to let it go because: (1) it is a fairly small amount given his net income of $500,000; and (2) families are welcome and encouraged to attend these conferences.

How would you advise the dentist? Would your conclusion be different if his wife and mother-in-law were the bookkeepers of the dental office? How about if he produced a brochure showing that child care is available for children?

Chart 6-2

ANSWERS TO QUESTIONS ON RETURNS

A member should make a reasonable effort to obtain from the taxpayer the information necessary to provide appropriate answers to all questions on a tax return before signing as preparer. (AICPA Statements on Standards for Tax Services 2)

The standard continues, "[t]he term **questions** includes requests for information on the return, in the instructions, or in the regulations, whether or not stated in the form of a question." Some questions are required to be answered, so a CPA must make an effort to obtain the information to be able to answer these questions. There also may be times when a CPA can legitimately omit an answer to a question on a return.

Recently, the number of questions on tax returns has grown, resulting in significantly complicating the completion and processing of a return. Some tax return questions have absolutely no bearing on computing the tax, the correctness of information on the return or anything to do with tax law.[2] In addition, many questions on returns, including those concerning entity ownership, have a relation to penalties that may be assessed. Some examples the standard uses for omitting an answer to a question include:

- the information is not readily available and the answer is not significant in terms of taxable income or loss, or the tax liability shown on the return;
- genuine uncertainty exists regarding the meaning of the question in relation to the particular return; and
- the answer to the question is voluminous; in such cases, a statement should be made on the return that the data will be supplied upon examination.

A CPA cannot omit an answer merely because it might prove disadvantageous to their client. What Would You Do 6-3 is a common situation.

WHAT WOULD YOU DO 6-3

Auto Questions

On the Federal Schedule "C" and Form 4562 there are questions regarding auto mileage. The questions are as follows:

a. Total business/investment miles driven during the year (don't include commuting miles)
b. Total commuting miles driven during the year
c. Total other personal (non-commuting) miles driven
d. Total miles driven during the year
e. Was the vehicle available for personal use during off-duty hours?
f. Was the vehicle used primarily by a more than 5% owner or related person?
g. Is another vehicle available for personal use?

Your client has given you the information to prepare the return but did not answer these questions on the questionnaire they provided. When you call, he says he really does not keep the number of miles but guesses that he drove about 15,000 during the year. When you ask how much of it

---

2. Examples of this are the governance questions in Part VI of Form 990.

is business related he answers, "All of it, of course. I use my wife's car for all non-business expenses."

Assume that your client is a pediatrician who lives eight miles from work. How would you handle this? Would your answer change if he drove a truck instead of a sedan? How about if he is an electrical contractor and this is his work truck?

Chart 6-3

CERTAIN PROCEDURAL ASPECTS OF PREPARING RETURNS

In preparing or signing a return, a member may in good faith rely, without verification, on information furnished by the taxpayer or by third parties. However, a member should not ignore the implications of information furnished and should make reasonable inquiries if the information furnished appears to be incorrect, incomplete, or inconsistent either on its face or on the basis of other facts known to the member. Further, a member should refer to the taxpayer's returns for one or more prior years whenever feasible.

If the tax law or regulations impose a condition with respect to deductibility or other tax treatment of an item, such as taxpayer maintenance of books and records or substantiating documentation to support the reported deduction or tax treatment, a member should make appropriate inquiries to determine to the member's satisfaction whether such condition has been met.

When preparing a tax return, a member should consider information actually known to that member from the tax return of another taxpayer if the information is relevant to that tax return and its consideration is necessary to properly prepare that tax return. In using such information, a member should consider any limitations imposed by any law or rule relating to confidentiality. (AICPA Statements on Standards for Tax Services 3)

When preparing returns, CPAs are given information from taxpayers and third parties, such as banks and brokerage houses. Given that there are so many sources, and different formats, how does the CPA know how much **due diligence**, verification and reliance is necessary?

For example, CPAs regularly receive information from various sources, such as Forms 1099 and Schedules K-1. Note that there is no requirement to audit this information, rather, this standard provides CPAs with the necessary steps to do this analysis and encourages obtaining supporting data where appropriate. The following are some examples:

- Unsupported data such as lists of tax information (i.e., dividends and interest received, charitable contributions, and medical expenses). While the CPA can use a list without additional verification if any of the items seems to be incorrect, incomplete or inconsistent, either on its face or on the basis of other facts known, to the CPA he or she should ask for clarification and, if necessary, supplementary information.
- Income and expenses related to security transactions and from pass-through entities, such as estates, trusts, partnerships, and S corporations. Due to the complexity of the tax laws, including basis issues and the forms themselves, reviewing the Form K-1 and attachments can be critical in obtaining and understanding all of the information.

It is suggested that, whenever feasible, the CPA review a client's returns for one or more prior years when preparing the current return. Reference to prior returns and discussion of prior-year tax issues with the client may help the CPA determine their general tax status, avoid the omission or duplication of items, locate loss and other carryforwards, and give the CPA a "road map" for the treatment of similar or related transactions. Keep in mind, depending on the client and their circumstances, comparison of the details of income and deduction between years might not be relevant.

The standard also recognizes that tax law is complicated, especially certain transactions and financial products. If any of these are bought and sold, it may require the CPA to obtain additional verification of these items. Sometimes obtaining the information may be tricky, as discussed in What Would You Do 6-4.

WHAT WOULD YOU DO 6-4

The First Distribution

GoGetUm is a new client who has been in business for ten years and has been a Subchapter "S" client since inception. The client gave you a schedule prepared by the prior CPA's tax software program with the title "Shareholder Basis Worksheet." There is a distribution from the corporation this year that, based on the schedule, may be in excess of their basis.

Can you rely on this form for the correct basis in preparing the current year's return? If not, what should you do?

Chart 6-4

USE OF ESTIMATES

Unless prohibited by statute or by rule, a member may use the taxpayer's estimates in the preparation of a tax return if it is not practical to obtain exact data and if the member determines that the estimates are reasonable based on the facts and circumstances known to the member. The taxpayer's estimates should be presented in a manner that does not imply greater accuracy than exists. (AICPA Statements on Standards for Tax Services 4)

When records are missing or precise information about a transaction is not available at the time the return must be filed, a CPA might have to prepare a tax return using the client's estimates of the missing data. The disclosure that an estimate is used for an item in the return is not generally required; however, a disclosure should be made in unusual circumstances where nondisclosure might mislead the taxing authority regarding the degree of accuracy of the return as a whole. Some examples of unusual circumstances include:

- a taxpayer has died or is ill;
- a taxpayer has not received a Schedule K-1 or 1099;
- there is pending litigation pending (e.g., a bankruptcy proceeding) that might have a bearing on the items on the return; and
- fire, computer failure, or a natural disaster has destroyed the relevant records.

What Would You Do 6-5 illustrates an example of how it may be difficult to obtain an estimate.

WHAT WOULD YOU DO 6-5

Home Office

Your client, a musician, has a separate room in her home office that she only uses to teach children and practice for recitals, so she qualifies for a home office deduction. She brings the actual expenses for the home but has not measured the floor space of the room used as an office. You ask her for an estimate and she says that this is one of three bedrooms. When asked about the total square footage, she thinks for a minute and estimates that the home office is about 300 square feet of 2,400 total square feet of the home.

In looking at her spreadsheet, the records of the actual expenses paid for her home during the year seem reasonable. Can you use the square footage estimate your client came up with? Is there anything else you might want to ask her prior to determining if this is something she can deduct?

Chart 6-5

DEPARTURE FROM A PREVIOUSLY CONCLUDED POSITION

The tax return position with respect to an item as determined in an administrative proceeding or court decision does not restrict a member from recommending a different tax position in a later year's return, unless the taxpayer is bound to a specified treatment in the later year, such as by a formal closing agreement. Therefore, the member may recommend a tax return position or prepare or sign a tax return that departs from the treatment of an item as concluded in an administrative proceeding or court decision with respect to a prior return of the taxpayer provided the requirements of Statement on Standards for Tax Services (SSTS) No. 1, Tax Return Positions, are satisfied. (AICPA Statements on Standards for Tax Services 5)

A CPA will generally be consistent in the treatment of items on tax returns, such as depreciable life or the allowance of certain deduction. If a tax audit or court decision determines a certain tax treatment of an item in a prior year's return is proper, the CPA will usually recommend this same tax treatment in subsequent years. There may be, however, occasions that may not be consistent. The following are some examples:

- In order to avoid litigation, the client agrees to an item during an audit. Just as the IRS is not bound to follow their previous ruling, the CPA's client is not bound to follow the tax treatment of this item as well.
- The audit decision was due to a lack of documentation. The client now has supporting data for the current year.
- Court decisions, rulings, or other authorities that are more favorable to the client's current position might have occurred since the prior proceeding was concluded or the prior court decision was rendered.

What Would You Do 6-6 presents a common illustration of how precedent may be used.

WHAT WOULD YOU DO 6-6
Learning the Hard Way

Your client is a real estate agent who was audited two years ago by the IRS. During the audit he was unable to substantiate the 20,000 business miles driven or the $9,500 conference he attended in Hawaii. He was assessed the tax and a penalty.

This year he comes to you to do his taxes, bringing a sheet that shows business miles driven broken down by day. You are surprised that this year his sheet says that he drove 32,000 business miles out of a total 35,000 total miles, even though the real estate market was slow and his income down 50%. In addition, he brought a program from a real estate convention in Miami and another spreadsheet with the costs incurred, including airfare, hotel and meals.

Keeping in mind that your client was audited and unable to substantiate the expenses in the audit, you ask if his records are better, and he says, "Of course." When you ask how they differ, he winks and says that he is "smarter" now.

How would you handle this situation? Would the auto deduction make a difference if he owned three cars?

Chart 6-6

KNOWLEDGE OF ERROR

A member should inform the taxpayer promptly upon becoming aware of an error in a previously filed return, an error in a return that is the subject of an administrative proceeding, or a taxpayer's failure to file a required return. A member also should advise the taxpayer of the potential consequences of the error and recommend the corrective measures to be taken. Such advice and recommendation may be given orally. The member is not allowed to inform the taxing authority without the taxpayer's permission, except when required by law.

If a member is requested to prepare the current year's return and the taxpayer has not taken appropriate action to correct an error in a prior year's return, the member should consider whether to withdraw from preparing the return and whether to continue a professional or employment relationship with the taxpayer. If the member does prepare such current year's return, the member should take reasonable steps to ensure that the error is not repeated.

If a member is representing a taxpayer in an administrative proceeding with respect to a return that contains an error of which the member is aware, the member should request the taxpayer's agreement to disclose the error to the taxing authority. Lacking such agreement, the member should consider whether to withdraw from representing the taxpayer in the administrative proceeding and whether to continue a professional or employment relationship with the taxpayer. (AICPA Statements on Standards for Tax Services 6)

While performing tax-related services, including preparation and representation in an audit, a CPA may find an error in a previously filed tax return or even discover that a required return was not filed. Once an error is discovered, this statement requires that the CPA let their client know about the error and the potential consequences, plus recommend any measures to rectify it. If an error is discovered in an audit or similar situation, the CPA should advise their client to disclose the error and the potential consequences of not disclosing the error. The advice and recommendation may be given either in writing or orally.

Discovery of errors are a fairly frequent occurrence, especially for returns that have not been filed. What Would You Do 6-7 demonstrates that situation.

WHAT WOULD YOU DO 6-7

An Unexpected Surprise

Your client, a small retail hobby shop, is getting audited by the IRS. The records are pristine, with great documentation, so you are not worried, until you look at a few sales invoices and discover that they are not collecting sales tax on internet sales made to customers in California, where the shop is located! These sales total about 30% of the gross income.

When you ask the owner of the business he gives you a puzzled look, explaining that customers don't want to pay sales tax on things they purchase online; in fact, that is why they buy it online, to save the tax. He has filed sales and use tax returns for years, and the company has never been audited.

How would you handle this situation? Would your answer change if some of the sales were out of state? How about if you prepared the quarterly sales tax returns for the last few years?

Note that it is the client's responsibility to decide whether to correct the error. If the client does not correct an error, either on the initial return or by filing an amended return, the CPA should consider whether to continue with the engagement or if there should even be a continuing relationship with the client. If the CPA believes there is potential fraud or other criminal misconduct, in order to preserve attorney-client privilege, the CPA should suggest that the client consult with an attorney.

This is not an issue just for CPAs in public practice. For a CPA in private industry who discovers an error and prepares an amended return, he or she must take "reasonable steps" to be sure that the error is not repeated. In both cases, public or private, if the error will not materially affect the client's tax liability, any action a CPA should take will be, based on the facts and circumstances, left to the CPA's professional judgment. This is illustrated in What Would You Do 6-8.

WHAT WOULD YOU DO 6-8

Amended Brokerage Information

It is April 10th and you transmitted the last tax returns, so it is time to relax and plan the next vacation. Just as you think about a few weeks in the sun, you receive an email from a client who received an amended Form 1099-DIV from his brokerage firm. You ask for a copy of the form, which includes this information:

	Original Amount	Correct Amount
Ordinary dividends	2,500	2,400
Qualified dividends	2,000	1,900
Capital gain dividends	4,000	4,200

Your client is petrified of an IRS audit and asks how to handle this. What would you advise them?

Chart 6-7

FORM AND CONTENT OF ADVICE TO TAXPAYERS

A member should use professional judgment to ensure that tax advice provided to a taxpayer reflects competence and appropriately serves the taxpayer's needs. When communicating tax advice to a taxpayer in writing, a member should comply with relevant taxing authorities' standards, if any, applicable to written tax advice. A member should use professional judgment about any need to document oral advice. A member is not required to follow a standard format when communicating or documenting oral advice.

A member should assume that tax advice provided to a taxpayer will affect the manner in which the matters or transactions considered would be reported or disclosed on the taxpayer's tax returns. Therefore, for tax advice given to a taxpayer, a member should consider, when relevant (a) return reporting and disclosure standards applicable to the related tax return position and (b) the potential penalty consequences of the return position. In ascertaining applicable return reporting and disclosure standards, a member should follow the standards in Statement on Standards for Tax Services No. 1, Tax Return Positions.

A member has no obligation to communicate with a taxpayer when subsequent developments affect advice previously provided with respect to significant matters, except while assisting a taxpayer in implementing procedures or plans associated with the advice provided or when a member undertakes this obligation by specific agreement. (AICPA Statements on Standards for Tax Services 7)

Many CPAs give tax advice, either oral or written, with the subject being anywhere from routine to complex. Because the range of advice is so extensive, and because the advice will always meet the specific situation and needs of a client, there is no standard format communicating or documenting the CPA's advice.

In routine matters or in well-defined areas, oral advice may be fine; however, written documentation and communication with the client is recommended in important, unusual, substantial dollar value, or complicated transactions. The standard gives these factors in deciding if the advice should be oral or written:

- The importance of the transaction and amounts involved
- The specific or general nature of the client's inquiry
- The time available for development and submission of the advice
- The technical complexity involved
- The existence of authorities and precedents
- The tax sophistication of the taxpayer
- The need to seek other professional advice
- The type of transaction and whether it is subject to heightened reporting or disclosure requirements
- The potential penalty consequences of the tax return position for which the advice is rendered
- Whether any potential applicable penalties can be avoided through disclosure
- Whether the member intends for the taxpayer to rely upon the advice to avoid potential penalties

What Would You Do 6-9 discusses how to handle the use of an expert.

WHAT WOULD YOU DO 6-9
Property Sale

A client has invested a substantial amount of money in the rehabilitation of a building with the intention of qualifying for rehabilitation and other available tax credits. The client is also interested in maximizing depreciation deductions and has asked you to prepare the tax returns for that year. Although you are an expert in real estate matters, you have never worked on this sort of transaction, but you have a friend who has. He agrees to help you determine depreciation lives of the building components and the tax benefits of the expenditures.

Is it necessary to tell your client that your friend will be helping? If so, exactly what should you tell your client about the need for outside expertise? Once the information comes back, how should you evaluate and document the advice you receive?

Federal Tax Rules

Circular 230[3] is an IRS publication containing the rules that govern the practice of licensed professionals before the IRS. These rules both encourage and prohibit certain conduct and impose penalties for those who are found to be in violation of the rules. Note that this does not just apply to CPAs but also attorneys, enrolled agents, enrolled actuaries, appraisers, and enrolled retirement plan agents.

In general, a tax preparer and advisor must exercise due diligence in preparing tax returns and providing tax advice. Circular 230 lists a set of best practices; the tax accountant must do the following:

- Provide the highest level of quality professional care, acting fairly and with integrity.
- Communicate clearly with the client so that the client's needs and expectations are understood.
- Establish the facts of the tax situation and then draw a conclusion consistent with the facts and the applicable tax laws.

---

3. Treasury Department Circular No. 230, Regulations Governing Practice before the Internal Revenue Service, June 2014, https://www.irs.gov/tax-professionals/circular-230-tax-professionals.

- Advise the client about the consequences of the conclusions reached and any potential penalties.
- Not advise the client to take a patently improper or frivolous position.
- Not charge "unconscionable" fees or charge contingency fees, except in a few restricted circumstances.
- Avoid conflicts of interests when representing more than one client.
- Not engage in false or misleading advertising or solicitation.
- Not cash IRS checks on behalf of clients.

Put simply, the CPA must ensure that tax returns and tax advice are based on realistic assessments. As illustrated in What Would you Do 6-10, the amounts claimed on tax returns cannot be frivolous.

WHAT WOULD YOU DO 6-10
The Tax Deduction

Your long-time client, an affluent physician, is planning on rebuilding his old house and putting up a new one on the same lot. In the planning process, the architect tells him about a program where the local fire department burns down old houses for training purposes. If your client donates the house, he can take a charitable deduction for the value of the building.

In preparing his taxes, your client presents you with an appraisal showing that the forty-five-year-old building is worth $450,000 and the land underneath is worth about the same. There is also a letter from the fire department thanking him for the donation and saying that they were able to salvage and sell about $10,000 worth of copper and other materials prior to torching the place.

This is a very affluent part of town, with mansions selling for over $1 million, so you wonder how legitimate the appraisal is. How would you handle this situation?

Only attorneys, CPAs, enrolled agents, enrolled actuaries, and/or enrolled retirement plan agents are allowed to represent their clients in IRS proceedings. **Representation** includes communication with the IRS regarding client matters, even when the client is not present. With proper authorization:

- an individual may represent a member of his or her immediate family;
- a regular full-time employee of an individual employer may represent the employer;
- a general partner or a regular full-time employee of a partnership may represent the partnership;
- a bona fide officer or a regular full-time employee of a corporation (including a parent, subsidiary, or other affiliated corporation), association, or organized group may represent the corporation, association, or organized group;
- a regular full-time employee of a trust, receivership, guardianship, or estate may represent the trust, receivership, guardianship, or estate;
- an officer or a regular employee of a governmental unit, agency, or authority may represent the governmental unit, agency, or authority in the course of his or her official duties; and
- an individual may represent any individual or entity, who is outside the United States, before personnel of the IRS when such representation takes place outside the United States.

Occasionally clients want to serve as their own advocate, as discussed in What Would You Do 6-11.

WHAT WOULD YOU DO 6-11

The Audit Letter

Gerry, a client of yours, prepared his own tax returns for thirty years until he finally decided to let a professional handle the chore, and you have done so for the last five years. One day you get a call from Gerry that he is being audited by the IRS. Having never been audited, he is upset and wants to know why.

He brings by a copy of the letter and it appears pretty routine, just documentation of charitable contributions. Gerry says he would like to handle this on his own but would like you to help him prepare for the audit.

How would you feel about helping Gerry in this way? Are there any reasons you might suggest you represent him?

Circular 230 also has some **required actions** that a CPA must follow. They include:

- disclosure of non-frivolous tax positions (frivolous tax positions are, of course, not allowed);
- returning records to clients;
- signing tax returns the CPA prepares;
- providing clients with a copy of their tax returns;
- advising clients of errors and omissions of either the client or the CPA;
- submitting records to the IRS in a timely manner; and
- the exercise of due diligence and use best practices governed by the profession.

During a busy time, you may inadvertently forget to sign a return. What Would You Do 6-12 illustrates this dilemma.

WHAT WOULD YOU DO 6-12

Forgot to Sign

A client who is located in another city calls you up and asks why you did not sign their corporate tax return, which is due tomorrow. You remember signing a bunch of them but must have missed this one. Naturally, the client waited until the last minute, including extensions, to let you know of this omission.

How would you handle this situation? How can you prevent it from happening in the future?

Tax shelters, also called **covered opinions**, are discussed in Circular 230. The CPA cannot provide advice that has tax avoidance or evasion as its principal purpose. However, they may issue a **reliance opinion**, which provides tax advice the CPA believes would probably be decided in the client's favor if questioned by the IRS. The CPA must ascertain the facts, make reasonable assumptions, and then come to a conclusion that not only is consistent with the law but also has a probable likelihood (better than 50% chance) of success.

Case 6-1

KPMG[4]

In the largest criminal tax case ever filed, KPMG admitted that it engaged in a fraud that generated at least $11 billion in phony tax losses that, according to court papers, cost the United States at least $2.5 billion in evaded taxes. In addition to KPMG's former deputy chairman, the individuals indicted included two former heads of KPMG's tax practice and a former tax partner in the New York office of a prominent national law firm.

The criminal information and indictment together alleged that, from 1996 through 2003, KPMG, the nine indicted defendants, and others conspired to defraud the IRS by designing, marketing and implementing illegal tax shelters. The charging documents focus on four shelters.

According to the charges, KPMG, the indicted individuals, and their co-conspirators concocted tax shelter transactions—together with false and fraudulent scenarios to support them—and targeted the shelters to wealthy individuals who needed at least $10 or $20 million in tax losses. These individuals would pay fees that were a percentage of the desired tax loss to KPMG, certain law firms, and others instead of paying the billions of dollars in taxes owed to the government. To further the scheme, KPMG, the individual defendants, and their co-conspirators filed false and fraudulent tax returns that claimed phony tax losses.

KPMG also admitted that its personnel took specific deliberate steps to conceal the existence of the shelters from the IRS by, among other things: failing to register the shelters with the IRS as required by law; fraudulently concealing the shelter losses and income on tax returns; and attempting to hide the shelters using sham attorney-client privilege claims. It also accused some of the defendants of lying to the IRS and to a Senate investigative panel during public hearings in November 2003.

In addition to the firm, a federal jury found three white-collar defendants guilty—two former employees and a former top tax lawyer. The verdicts, on multiple counts of tax evasion, were the result of the government spending more than three years prosecuting its case against an original group of nineteen defendants,

---

4. Internal Revenue Service, "KPMG to Pay $456 Million for Criminal Violations," *IRS.gov*, *August 29, 2005, https://www.irs.gov/newsroom/kpmg-to-pay-456-million-for-criminal-violations. Jonathan Weil, "Nine Are Charged in KPMG Case on Tax Shelters," Wall Street Journal, August 30, 2005, https://www.wsj.com/articles/SB112533172910025699.*

seventeen of them from KPMG.

Internal Revenue **Code Section 7216** prohibits a tax preparer from "knowingly or recklessly" disclosing or using tax return information; a violation of this section could result in a preparer's being charged with a criminal misdemeanor. In addition, **Code Section 6713** imposes a penalty for the unauthorized disclosure or use of tax return information. These penalties are included in Chart 6-8.

Under the regulations, a tax preparer must usually get permission—in writing or electronically—from their client before disclosing or using information on the tax return. The regulations also specify the form and content of the disclosure, which are different on individual and other returns.

There are exceptions to this rule, such as disclosure under a court order or using the information when preparing state and local tax returns or estimated tax vouchers. Also, responding to a request for information by providing it to the IRS is allowed. There are other permissible disclosures or uses included in the regulations.

Most banks and other lenders ask for verification of certain information prior to approving or funding a loan. What Would You Do 6-13 is a common situation.

WHAT WOULD YOU DO 6-13

Mortgage Inquiry

You receive a phone call from a mortgage broker who your client, a self-employed attorney, has used in the past to refinance his house. The broker indicates that your client is purchasing a new house and, while he already has copies of the last three years' tax returns, he needs some information today in order to package the loan. While you are talking, you receive an email asking for the following:

1. A statement that the client is self-employed and the number of years of self-employment
2. The amount of income from self-employment
3. Ownership percentage of the business entity
4. Explanation of the profitability of the business
5. Effect on the business if money is used for the purchase being financed

How would you handle this request? If your client had called first, would your response be any different? How about if the broker asked you for copies of the returns in addition to the above?

Tax Fraud

Income **tax fraud** is commonly defined as "the willful attempt to evade tax law or defraud the government." Some examples of tax fraud include:

- intentionally failing to file a tax return;
- willfully failing to pay taxes due;
- intentionally failing to report all income received;
- making fraudulent or false claims; and
- preparing and filing a false return.

The US tax code is so complicated that most people, including some professionals, do not understand much of it. Unless there are signs of fraud, the IRS will usually assume it was an honest mistake rather than willful evasion and will generally consider it a mistake rather than fraud. Even though it may have not been intentional, the IRS can still impose a penalty of 20% of the underpayment.

Some common types of suspicious and fraudulent activity are:

- overstating deductions;
- concealing or transferring income;
- keeping two sets of books;
- deducting personal expenses as business expenses;
- using a fake Social Security number; and
- willfully underreporting income.

Since cash is easy to hide, those who are paid mostly in cash and self-employed taxpayers in cash-based businesses have been identified as those who commit the most fraud. Restaurants, car dealers, salespeople, doctors, lawyers, accountants, and hairdressers were ranked as the top offenders in a government study of income tax fraud.

Case 6-2

DONALD BIAGI, JR[5].

Donald Biagi provided landscaping and snowplowing services to commercial and residential customers. Instead of depositing all of the gross receipts into his business bank accounts, Biagi would go to the bank and cash client checks. Between 2008 and 2010, he cashed approximately 574 client checks, ranging in amounts from $10.52 to $15,604.50.

Biagi was his own bookkeeper who did not tell his tax return preparer about the client checks he cashed. As a result, a total of $1,321,305 in business gross receipts were not reported on his federal tax returns for three years, meaning he substantially underreported his taxable income. The amount of unreported income was about 62% of his business's gross receipts in 2008, 47% of the gross receipts in 2009, and 60% of the gross receipts in 2010.

Biagi was sentenced to eighteen months in prison and one year of supervised release and was ordered to pay $445,579 in back taxes, plus penalties and interest that accrued on the unpaid taxes.

Tax Preparer Penalties

In addition to professional and state penalties, the Internal Revenue Code has many sections devoted to **tax preparer penalties**. Chart 6-8 summarizes many of them:[6]

---

5. US Department of Justice, US Attorney's Office, District of Connecticut, Fairfield County Landscaper Pleads Guilty to Tax Evasion, September 29, 2016, https://www.justice.gov/usao-ct/pr/fairfield-county-landscaper-pleads-guilty-tax-evasion.
6. Summary of Preparer Penalties under Title 26, https://www.irs.gov/tax-professionals/summary-of-preparer-penalties-under-title-26. Note that these penalties are periodically revised by statute.

Chart 6-8

FEDERAL TAX PENALTIES

IRC § 6694(a) – **Understatement due to unreasonable positions.** The penalty is the greater of $1,000 or 50% of the income derived by the tax return preparer with respect to the return or claim for refund.

IRC § 6694(b) – **Understatement due to willful or reckless conduct.** The penalty is the greater of $5,000 or 50% of the income derived by the tax return preparer with respect to the return or claim for refund.

IRC § 6695(a) – **Failure to furnish copy to taxpayer.** The penalty is $50 for each failure to comply with IRC § 6107 regarding furnishing a copy of a return or claim to a taxpayer, up to $25,500 in a calendar year.

IRC § 6695(b) – **Failure to sign return.** The penalty is $50 for each failure to sign a return or claim for refund as required by regulations, up to $25,500 in a calendar year.

IRC § 6695(c) – **Failure to furnish identifying number.** The penalty is $50 for each failure to comply with IRC § 6109(a)(4) regarding furnishing an identifying number on a return or claim, up to $25,500 in a calendar year.

IRC § 6695(d) – **Failure to retain copy or list.** The penalty is $50 for each failure to comply with IRC § 6107(b) regarding retaining a copy or list of a return or claim, up to $25,500 in a return period.

IRC § 6695(e) – **Failure to file correct information returns.** The penalty is $50 for each failure to comply with IRC § 6060, up to $25,500 in a return period.

IRC § 6695(f) – **Negotiation of check.** The penalty is $510 for a tax return preparer who endorses or negotiates any check which is issued to a taxpayer.

IRC § 6695(g) – **Failure to be diligent in determining eligibility for earned income credit.** The penalty is $510 for each failure to comply with the EIC due diligence requirements imposed in regulations.

IRC § 6700 – **Promoting abusive tax shelters.** The penalty is for a promoter of an abusive tax shelter and is generally equal to $1,000 for each organization or sale of an abusive plan or arrangement (or, if lesser, 100% of the income derived from the activity).

IRC § 6701 - **Penalties for aiding and abetting understatement of tax liability.** The penalty is $1,000 ($10,000 if the conduct relates to a corporation's tax return) for aiding and abetting in an understatement of a tax liability.

IRC § 6713 - **Disclosure or use of information by preparers of returns.** The penalty is $250 for each unauthorized disclosure or use of information furnished for, or in connection with, the preparation of a return, up to $10,000 in a calendar year.

IRC § 7206 - **Fraud and false statements.** Guilty of a felony and, upon conviction, a fine of not more than $100,000 ($500,000 in the case of a corporation), imprisonment of not more than three years, or both (together with the costs of prosecution).

IRC § 7207 - **Fraudulent returns, statements, or other documents.** Guilty of a misdemeanor and, upon conviction, a fine of not more than $10,000 ($50,000 in the case of a corporation), imprisonment of not more than one year, or both.

IRC § 7216 - **Disclosure or use of information by preparers of returns.** Guilty of a misdemeanor for knowingly or recklessly disclosing information furnished in connection with a tax return or using such information for any purpose other than preparing or assisting in the preparation of such return. Upon conviction, a fine of not more than $1,000, imprisonment for not more than 1 year, or both (together with the costs of prosecution).

Discussion Questions

1. Under what circumstances should you refuse to provide professional services to an individual tax client?

2. When can a CPA tax return preparer rely upon information furnished by a client?

3. How do you know when there is "substantial authority" for a tax return position? What if there is none?

4. When should a CPA refrain from claiming estimated deductions on a client's tax return?

5. What are some of the practical problems associated with applying the "reasonable basis" standard?

6. When should a tax return preparer advocate for a client? If tax return preparers were permitted to solely act as advocates for their clients' interests, without regard to the public interest, what would be the consequences?

7. Describe three ethical duties that apply to tax return preparers.

8. Describe three ethical duties that apply to CPAs who provide tax planning services to their clients.

9. Should a CPA tax return preparer have a duty to verify the information provided to them by clients? Why or why not?

10. What are a CPA's duties, if any, upon discovering an error in a tax return that he prepared? How about a tax return prepared by another accountant?

11. What is tax fraud? How can you detect it? If you suspect tax fraud, what should you do?

12. Which of the federal tax penalties do you think are assessed the most? How do you think they can be avoided?

13. Jim, your tax client, brings you a prospectus on a new investment idea that also has significant tax benefits. It is a pretty thick book and, as you go through it, there is a letter from a local law firm that describes the tax benefits based on a Code section you have never heard of and a case that seems a bit "out there."

    a. What steps should you take before advising Jim as to whether the tax benefits which are claimed in the prospectus are legitimate?
    b. If you conclude that the position is bogus and Jim invests against your advice, how does that impact you when preparing future tax returns for Jim?

14. Your brother-in-law owns a car wash and is unhappy with his CPA's client service. Naturally, you are asked to help and, to keep peace in the family, agree to prepare his corporate and personal tax returns. As he brings you the information, you are shocked to see that the business nets only $50,000 per year, yet you know he has three new cars, a huge house and consistently buys your sister expensive jewelry.

    a. How would you handle this situation?
    b. Do you have any legal or professional responsibilities to investigate?

15. Your client, a real estate agent, receives Form 1099-MISC from his broker every year, which is reported as the gross receipts from his business. Another client of yours shows that they pay a management fee directly to your client every month. When you ask to see the check, you notice it is made out to the agent, not the broker, and endorsed by him.

    a. How would you handle this situation?
    b. Do you have any legal or professional responsibilities to investigate?

Case Study[7]

Charles and Mary Bangle bought a controlling interest in Manco & Manco Pizza, which had previously been known as Mack & Manco. The chain consists of three stores on the boardwalk in Ocean City and a location in Somers Point. Charles ran day-to-day operations, and Mary handled the cash and payroll.

Charles failed to report $263,113 in income, avoiding more than $91,000 in taxes. He also admitted making cash deposits of less than $10,000 to avoid federal reporting requirements.

Mary admitted that she lied when she told IRS agents that she deposited just enough of the cash receipts to meet payroll and other expenses, when she was actually using undeposited cash for personal expenses. She also lied about the amount of money she deposited into her personal bank account.

Charles was ordered to pay restitution of $248,560, serve a fifteen-month prison term and also pay a $5,000 fine. Mary was sentenced to three years of probation and fined $3,000.

---

7. USA v. Bangle et al., New Jersey District Court, Case No. 1:14-cr-00174, September 2, 2015.

Case Study Questions

1. Do you believe their CPA may have known about this fraud? If so, give your reasons. If not, what might have tipped him off?

2. Do you believe the punishment by the court was adequate? Was the sentence too light? Or not severe enough? Why do you feel this way?

3. Describe the specific tax preparer penalties, including the Code sections, that might have been imposed by the IRS.

CHAPTER 7

CALIFORNIA ETHICS RULES

Government does not tax to get the money it needs; government always finds a need for the money it gets.

—*Ronald Reagan, former governor of California and 40th president (1911–2004)*

Every state has its own rules governing licensed accountants, and California is no exception. The **California Board of Accountancy** is responsible for regulating the accounting profession with its licensure and enforcement programs. This chapter will look at selected sections of the California Accountancy Act and Regulations, highlighting their effect on the practice of accounting in California.[1]

You will note that many of the laws and regulations are similar to the AICPA rules, but there is one important difference. If you violate the AICPA rules, you can be expelled from the association; if you violate the board of accountancy rules and regulations, you can be fined and potentially lose your license!

---

1. References in this chapter are from the California Accountancy Act and Regulations, http://www.dca.ca.gov/cba/about-cba/accountancy-act.shtml.

California Accountancy Act

The California Accountancy Act consists of a group of laws which have been passed by the legislature and signed by the Governor. The Act is summarized below:

Article 1—Administration: Similar to bylaws in a corporation, this article discusses the nature of the Board, their duties, the various committees and similar items.

Article 1.5—Continuing Education: Discusses the statutory continuing education requirements and committee.

Article 2—General Powers and Definitions: Defines various terms used in the Act.

Article 3—Application of Chapter: Describes who is covered under the Act, including defining CPA, plus authorizes inactive and retired designations.

Article 3.5—Standards of Professional Conduct: Sets out the rules for naming an accounting firm, discusses commissions, professional standards and reportable events.

Article 4—Applications, Registrations, Permits Generally: Sets forth requirements for certificates of both individuals and firms, discusses peer review and non-licensee ownership of firms.

Article 5—Certificates, Information and Records: Describes the rules necessary to qualify for a CPA license in California.

Article 5.1—Practice Privileges: Contains rules for accountants from other jurisdictions who may want to practice accounting in California.

Article 5.5—Audit Documentation: Describes audit documentation requirements and provides the authority for regulations to implement these rules.

Article 6—Disciplinary Proceedings: Discusses the role of the Board in investigating violations of the rules, including various definitions and petitions.

Article 6.5—Administrative penalties: Provides the authorization to charge penalties for various violations of the rules.

Article 7—Prohibitions and Offenses Against the Chapter Generally: Provides authorization for the Board to charge certain violations as a crime.

Article 8—Revenue: Discusses the fees the Board can charge.

Article 9—Accountancy Corporations: Spells out the rules that apply to Accountancy Corporations.

Accountancy Regulations

California Board of Accountancy Regulations are rules passed by the Board to implement the Accountancy Act. Some of the areas covered are:

Article 1—General: Discusses various definitions and the requirement to notify the board of accountancy of any change of address.

Article 2—Examinations: Discusses the various requirements for taking and passing the CPA exam in California.

Article 6—Peer Review: Spells out the requirements for obtaining a peer review, including who is covered and exclusions.

Article 9—Rules of Professional Conduct: Details the specific rules, some of which are discussed in the next section.

Article 12—Continuing Education Rules: Sets out the requirements for continuing education, including which programs qualify, what must be taken and how to report.

Article 12.5—Citations and Fines: Discusses the citations and fines that can be imposed, including the appeals process.

Article 13—Denial, Suspensions, and Revocation of Certificates, Permits or Licenses: Provides the guidelines for disciplinary action, including rehabilitation criteria.

Specific Areas

While the above descriptions are general in nature, there are a number of practical areas discussed below:

- Accountant Designations (Chart 7-1)
- Fees and Commissions (Chart 7-2)
- Reporting Requirements (Chart 7-3)
- Reporting Restatements (Chart 7-4)
- Peer Review (Chart 7-5)
- Non-licensee Owners of Accounting Firms (Chart 7-6)
- Audit Documentation (Chart 7-7)
- Confidential Information Defined (Chart 7-8)
- Disclosure of Confidential Information (Chart 7-9)
- Record Retention (Chart 7-10)
- Working Papers (Chart 7-11)

Chart 7-1

ACCOUNTANT DESIGNATIONS

No person or partnership shall assume or use the title or designation "chartered accountant," "certified accountant," "enrolled accountant," "registered accountant" or "licensed accountant," or any other title or designation likely to be confused with "certified public accountant" or "public accountant," or any of the abbreviations "C.A.," "E.A.," "R.A.," or "L.A.," or similar abbreviations likely to be confused with "C.P.A." or "P.A."; provided, that any person qualified as a certified public accountant under this chapter who also holds a comparable title granted under the laws of another country may use such title in conjunction with the title of "certified public accountant" or "C.P.A." and provided, that any person enrolled to practice before the Internal Revenue Service and recognized as an enrolled agent may use the abbreviation "E.A." (California Accountancy Act and Regulations §5058).

A person or firm may not use any title or designation in connection with the designation "certified public accountant" or "public accountant" that is false or misleading. (California Accountancy Act and Regulations §5058.1)

While these rules seem pretty straightforward, What Would You Do 7-1 looks at how these rules may be applied in a practical situation.

WHAT WOULD YOU DO 7-1

Starting Your Business

You graduated from college, passed the CPA exam, met the necessary experience requirement, and the paperwork is waiting to be approved by the California Board of Accountancy. Even though you had no intention of starting your own practice so soon, several of your friends have businesses that need financial statement audits, which is what you have been doing for your employer! Their banks need the final audits in the next thirty days, and you can take time off to complete them.

How would you handle this situation?

Chart 7-2

FEES AND COMMISSIONS

(a) Except as expressly permitted by this section, a person engaged in the practice of public accountancy shall not: (1) pay a fee or commission to obtain a client or (2) accept a fee or commission for referring a client to the products or services of a third party.

(b) A person engaged in the practice of public accountancy who is not performing any of the services set forth in subdivision (c) and who complies with the disclosure requirements of subdivision (d) may accept a fee or commission for providing a client with the products or services of a third party where the products or services of a third party are provided in conjunction with professional services provided to the client by the person engaged in the practice of public accountancy. Nothing in this subdivision shall be construed to permit the solicitation or acceptance of any fee or commission solely for the referral of a client to a third party.

(c) A person engaged in the practice of public accountancy is prohibited from performing services for a client, or an officer or director of a client, or a client-sponsored retirement plan, for a commission or from receiving a commission from a third party for providing the products or services of that third party to a client, or an officer or director of a client, or a client-sponsored retirement plan, during the period in which the person also performs for that client, or officer or director of that client, or client-sponsored retirement plan, any of the services listed below and during the period covered by any historical financial statements involved in those listed services:

    (1) An audit or review of a financial statement.

    (2) A compilation of a financial statement when that person expects, or reasonably might expect, that a third party will use the financial statement and the compilation report does not disclose a lack of independence.

    (3) An examination of prospective financial information.

(d) A person engaged in the practice of public accountancy who is not prohibited from performing services for a commission, or from receiving a commission, and who is paid or expects to be paid a commission, shall disclose that fact to any client or entity to whom the person engaged in the practice of public accountancy recommends or refers a product or service to which the commission relates. (excerpt from California Accountancy Act and Regulations §5061)

As illustrated in Case 7-1, any CPA who accepts or plans to accept a fee or commission should be familiar with the rules found in Chart 7-2.

Case 7-1

ANDREW KEEDUCK JEAN[2]

Over a four year period, Jean received $114,928.60 for referring clients to XYZ Asset Management Inc. and/or ABC Investments, Inc. and made no related disclosures as required under Section 5061 of the Accountancy Act. Jean also issued unaudited financial statements to clients without providing either a compilation report or an engagement letter containing appropriate elements as required by professional standards.

He was charged with violating, among other things, §5061. His license was suspended for three months, he was put on three years' probation and ordered to complete eight hours of continuing education in addition to the continuing education required for license renewal. Jean also paid an administrative penalty of $2,500 and reimbursed the California Board of Accountancy $13,874.41 for their investigation and prosecution costs.

Chart 7-3

REPORTING REQUIREMENTS

(a) A licensee shall report to the board in writing of the occurrence of any of the following events occurring on or after January 1, 1997, within 30 days of the date the licensee has knowledge of these events:

    (1) The conviction of the licensee of any of the following:

        (A) A felony.

        (B) Any crime related to the qualifications, functions, or duties of a public accountant or certified public accountant, or to acts or activities in the course and scope of the practice of public accountancy.

        (C) Any crime involving theft, embezzlement, misappropriation of funds or property, breach of a fiduciary responsibility,

---

2. California Board of Accountancy, Accusation No. AC-2011-5, April 28, 2012.

or the preparation, publication, or dissemination of false, fraudulent, or materially misleading financial statements, reports, or information.

As used in this section, a conviction includes the initial plea, verdict, or finding of guilt, pleas of no contest, or pronouncement of sentence by a trial court even though that conviction may not be final or sentence actually imposed until appeals are exhausted.

(2)   The cancellation, revocation, or suspension of a certificate, other authority to practice or refusal to renew a certificate or other authority to practice as a certified public accountant or a public accountant, by any other state or foreign country.

(3)   The cancellation, revocation, or suspension of the right to practice as a certified public accountant or a public accountant before any governmental body or agency.

(b)   A licensee shall report to the board in writing the occurrence of any of the following events occurring on or after January 1, 2003, within 30 days of the date the licensee has knowledge of the events:

(1)   Any restatement of a financial statement and related disclosures by a client audited by the licensee.

(2)   Any civil action settlement or arbitration award against the licensee relating to the practice of public accountancy where the amount or value of the settlement or arbitration award is thirty thousand dollars ($30,000) or greater and where the licensee is not insured for the full amount of the award.

(3)   Any notice of the opening or initiation of a formal investigation of the licensee by the Securities and Exchange Commission or its designee.

(4)   Any notice from the Securities and Exchange Commission to a licensee requesting a Wells Submission.

(5)   Any notice of the opening or initiation of an investigation by the Public Company Accounting Oversight Board or its designee, as defined pursuant to subdivision (g).

(c) A licensee shall report to the board in writing, within 30 days of the entry of the judgment, any judgment entered on or after January 1, 2003, against the licensee in any civil action alleging any of the following:

(1)   Dishonesty, fraud, gross negligence, or negligence.

(2)   Breach of fiduciary responsibility.

> (3) Preparation, publication, or dissemination of false, fraudulent, or materially misleading financial statements, reports, or information.
>
> (4) Embezzlement, theft, misappropriation of funds or property, or obtaining money, property, or other valuable consideration by fraudulent means or false pretenses, or other errors or omissions.
>
> (5) Any actionable conduct by the licensee in the practice of public accountancy, the performance of bookkeeping operations, or other professional practice. (excerpt from California Accountancy Act and Regulations §5063)

Case 7-2 illustrates what can happen when these rules are not followed.

Case 7-2

STERLING BLAIR ABERNATHY[3]

The SEC complaint alleged that Abernathy, while employed at IMB, Inc. as an executive vice president and chief financial officer, negligently made materially false and misleading statements regarding the quality of the residential mortgage loans underlying the offerings during the offer and sale of six IndyMac Mortgage-backed securities. The SEC complaint also alleged that Abernathy negligently made false and misleading statements regarding IndyMac's capital and liquidity position in its common stock prospectus filed on May 2, 2008. IndyMac filed for Chapter 7 bankruptcy on or about July 31, 2008.

There was a final judgment by the SEC in which Abernathy was ordered to pay disgorgement of $25,000, prejudgment interest of $1,592.26, and a civil penalty in the amount of $100,000. In addition, they suspended him from appearing or practicing before the SEC as an accountant.

Abernathy failed to report his investigation by the SEC to the California Board of Accountancy within thirty days of notice.

Among other things, he was charged with violating California Accountancy Act and Regulations §5063 (b)(3). He agreed to surrender his CPA license and reimburse the board of accountancy $5,176 for its investigation and prosecution costs should he ever want to reinstate his CPA certificate.

---

3. California Board of Accountancy, Accusation 2012-31, September 1, 2012.

There are occasions when financial statements are issued and later found out to be incorrect. Chart 7-4 discusses the reporting responsibilities in these instances and What Would You Do 7-2 poses a practical question.

Chart 7-4

REPORTING RESTATEMENTS

(a) To comply with the requirements of paragraph (1) of subdivision (b) of Business and Professions Code Section 5063, a licensee who issues a report on a client's restated financial statement shall report to the Board:

    (1) Any restatement of a financial statement reporting the correction of any error in a previously issued financial statement of a client that is a government agency located in California, when the financial restatement(s) exceeds the planning materiality used by the licensee in conjunction with the current year audit. For purposes of this paragraph, planning materiality means the planned level of misstatements, individually or in aggregate, that would cause the financial statements to not be presented fairly, in all material respects, in conformity with generally accepted accounting principles.

    (2) Any restatement of a financial statement of a charitable organization registered by the Office of the Attorney General's Registry of Charitable Trusts which is issued for purposes of correcting any error in a previously issued financial statement and which has resulted in the filing of an amended or superseding Internal Revenue Service Form 990 of 990PF.

(b) The report required by subsection (a) shall be made by the licensee issuing the report on the restatement even if the licensee did not perform the original audit. (California Accountancy Act and Regulations §59)

WHAT WOULD YOU DO 7-2

Nonprofit Audit

You have just been elected to the board of a charity that obtains an annual financial statement audit. As you look at their accounting for restricted gifts, you cannot help but notice they have not been following GAAP in the past. After asking some questions, it is obvious that the CPA did not understand the rules for nonprofits, and the board decides to engage another firm to perform the following year's audit.

What factors should you consider prior to deciding if you recommend restating the prior year's financial statements and reporting this to the board of accountancy, as opposed to simply showing the difference in the current year's financial statements as a prior period adjustment? Would your answer be different if the IRS audited the client and asked about the adjustment?

Both the AICPA and the California Board of Accountancy have requirements for many CPA's to have a peer review. Chart 7-5 describes the California law.

Chart 7-5

PEER REVIEW

(a) In order to renew its registration in an active status or convert to an active status, a firm, as defined in Section 5035.1, shall have a peer review report of its accounting and auditing practice accepted by a board-recognized peer review program no less frequently than every three years.

(b) For purposes of this article, the following definitions apply:

   (1) "Peer review" means a study, appraisal, or review conducted in accordance with professional standards of the professional work of a firm and may include an evaluation of other factors in accordance with the requirements specified by the board in regulations. The peer review report shall be issued by an individual who has a valid and current license, certificate, or permit to practice public accountancy from this state or another state and is unaffiliated with the firm being reviewed.

(2) "Accounting and auditing practice" includes any services that were performed in the prior three years using professional standards defined by the board in regulations.

(c) The board shall adopt regulations as necessary to implement, interpret, and make specific the peer review requirements in this section, including, but not limited to, regulations specifying the requirements for board recognition of a peer review program, standards for administering a peer review, extensions of time for fulfilling the peer review requirement, exclusions from the peer review program, and document submission.

(d) Nothing in this section shall prohibit the board from initiating an investigation and imposing discipline against a firm or licensee, either as the result of a complaint that alleges violations of statutes, rules, or regulations, or from information contained in a peer review report received by the board.

(e) A firm issued a substandard peer review report, as defined by the board in regulation, shall submit a copy of that report to the board. The board shall establish in regulation the time period that a firm must submit the report to the board. This period shall not exceed 60 days from the time the report is accepted by a board-recognized peer review program provider to the date the report is submitted to the board. (excerpt from California Accountancy Act and Regulations §5076)

Peer reviews are designed to enhance the quality of accounting, auditing, and attestation services and to help CPAs provide high-quality accounting services. The board of accountancy has additional regulations explaining who they apply to, how the reviews work, and as details regarding reporting and other items.[4]

---

4. For the most up-to-date rules, Article 6 of the California Board of Accountancy regulations should be reviewed. They can be found at http://www.dca.ca.gov/cba/about-cba/regulations.shtml.

Case 7-3

IRENE T. JEWELL[5]

Jewell performed audits of the NCTI Defined Benefit Plan (the Plan) for two years. The audits were subject to Generally Accepted Auditing Standards (GAAS), GAAP, and ERISA. Jameson committed acts of gross negligence due to the extreme departures from GAAS, ERISA and the standard of care.

Jewell's acts included failures to obtain an understanding of the engagement through a written communication, to properly plan the audit, and to obtain a sufficient understanding of the Plan to assess risks. Jewell did not: assess and document materiality; obtain sufficient evidential matter; perform cut-off procedures; or perform analytical review procedures. Jewell failed to apply and document auditing procedures to the individual participant accounts. Jewell's audit documentation and audit reports failed to comply with professional standards; her audit documentation did not support her unqualified opinion rendered in the audit report. She also failed to obtain a peer review.

Jewell was charged with violating, among others, §5076(a). She was put on three years' probation, during which time she could not perform any attest engagements, except for compilations, and after which she could not do without the permission of the board of accountancy. She also had to have a peer review, complete continuing education and reimburse the board $14,459.60 for its investigation and prosecution costs.

Like most states, California seeks to keep the controlling interest in accounting firms in the hands of licensees. Their stated goal is that this will, by regulating the professional, encourage high-quality professional services instead of low-quality or substandard work in an effort to generate the most revenue. Chart 7-6 describes ownership requirements of CPA firms.

5. California Board of Accountancy, Accusation Number 2013-41, August 31, 2014.

Chart 7-6

NON-LICENSEE OWNERS OF ACCOUNTING FIRMS

(a) Notwithstanding any other provision of this chapter, any firm lawfully engaged in the practice of public accountancy in this state may have owners who are not licensed as certified public accountants or public accountants if the following conditions are met:

(1) Non-licensee owners shall be natural persons or entities, such as partnerships, professional corporations, or others, provided that each ultimate beneficial owner of an equity interest in that entity shall be a natural person materially participating in the business conducted by the firm or an entity controlled by the firm.

(2) Non-licensee owners shall materially participate in the business of the firm, or an entity controlled by the firm, and their ownership interest shall revert to the firm upon the cessation of any material participation.

(3) Licensees shall in the aggregate, directly or beneficially, comprise a majority of owners, except that firms with two owners may have one owner who is a non-licensee.

(4) Licensees shall in the aggregate, directly or beneficially, hold more than half of the equity capital and possess majority voting rights.

(5) Non-licensee owners shall not hold themselves out as certified public accountants or public accountants and each licensed firm shall disclose actual or potential involvement of non-licensee owners in the services provided.

(6) There shall be a certified public accountant or public accountant who has ultimate responsibility for each financial statement attest and compilation service engagement.

(7) Except as permitted by the board in the exercise of its discretion, a person may not become a non-licensee owner or remain a non-licensee owner if the person has done either of the following:

(A) Been convicted of any crime, an element of which is dishonesty or fraud, under the laws of any state, of the United States, or of any other jurisdiction.

(B) Had a professional license or the right to practice revoked or suspended for reasons other than nonpayment of dues or fees, or has voluntarily surrendered a license or right to practice with disciplinary charges or a disciplinary investigation pending, and not reinstated by a licensing or regulatory agency of any state, or of the United States, including, but not limited to, the Securities and Exchange Commission or Public Company Accounting Oversight Board, or of any other jurisdiction. (excerpt from California Accountancy Act and Regulations §5079)

What Would You Do 7-3 looks at applying these rules in a common situation.

WHAT WOULD YOU DO 7-3

Three Good Friends

Your friend needs help. He has started a CPA firm and is swamped; who knew that forensic accounting could be so time-consuming? You have just passed the CPA exam and are looking for a job, and this sounds terrific since he offered that the two of you would immediately become partners and share all profits 50/50. He is also thinking of having another friend, an attorney, join the business as an equal partner; there is plenty of money to go around!

According to the board of accountancy rules, can you become a partner with your friend and split the profits 50/50? How about if the attorney joins the firm at the same time? Can you come up with any alternatives that might work?

Both the AICPA and the California Board of Accountancy have rules regarding audit documentation. The California requirements are spelled out in Chart 7-7.

Chart 7-7

AUDIT DOCUMENTATION

(a) Audit documentation shall be a licensee's records of the procedures applied, the tests performed, the information obtained, and the pertinent conclusions reached in an audit engagement. Audit documentation shall include, but is not limited to, programs, analyses, memoranda, letters of confirmation and representation, copies or abstracts of company documents, and schedules or commentaries prepared or obtained by the licensee.

(b) Audit documentation shall contain sufficient documentation to enable a reviewer with relevant knowledge and experience, having no previous connection with the audit engagement, to understand the nature, timing, extent, and results of the auditing or other procedures performed, evidence obtained, and conclusions reached, and to determine the identity of the persons who performed and reviewed the work.

(c) Failure of the audit documentation to document the procedures applied, tests performed, evidence obtained, and relevant conclusions reached in an engagement shall raise a presumption that the procedures were not applied, tests were not performed, information was not obtained, and relevant conclusions were not reached. This presumption shall be a rebuttable presumption affecting the burden of proof relative to those portions of the audit that are not documented as required in subdivision (b). The burden may be met by a preponderance of the evidence.

(d) Audit documentation shall be maintained by a licensee for the longer of the following:

(1) The minimum period of retention provided in subdivision (e).

(2) A period sufficient to satisfy professional standards and to comply with applicable laws and regulations.

(e) Audit documentation shall be maintained for a minimum of seven years which shall be extended during the pendency of any board investigation, disciplinary action, or legal action involving the licensee or the licensee's firm. The board may adopt regulations to

> establish a different retention period for specific categories of audit documentation where the board finds that the nature of the documentation warrants it.
>
> (f) Licensees shall maintain a written documentation retention and destruction policy that shall set forth the licensee's practices and procedures complying with this article. (California Accountancy Act and Regulations §5097)

If you believe that paragraph (b) in Chart 7-7 is vague, you are not alone. Since there is no real definition of standard audit documentation, good luck defining "adequate".

Case 7-4

MAYER HOFFMAN MCCANN P.C.[6]

Mayer Hoffman McCann P.C. was the independent auditor for the City of Bell for five years. On the 2009 audit for the City of Bell and the Bell Community Redevelopment Agency, the firm departed from professional standards, including failure to properly perform risk assessments and failure to document performance of certain minimum procedures to comply with compliance testing requirements. In addition, the firm insufficiently documented their audit procedures for the City of Bell and the Bell Community Redevelopment Agency.

The firm agreed to a violation of §5097. Their license was revoked, but they were allowed to continue in business with two years' probation. They also were required to undergo peer review, attend governmental training sessions, reimburse the board of accountancy up to $50,000 for its investigation and prosecution costs and pay an administrative fine of $300,000.

Chart 5-12 spelled out the AICPA rules regarding confidential information; Charts 7-8 and 7-9 discuss the California requirements.

---

6. California Board of Accountancy, Accusation Number 2012-17, December 26, 2012.

Chart 7-8

CONFIDENTIAL INFORMATION DEFINED

"Confidential information" includes all information obtained by a licensee, in his or her professional capacity, concerning a client or a prospective client, except that it does not include information obtained from a prospective client who does not subsequently become a client, where all of the following conditions are met:

(a) The licensee provides reasonable notice to the prospective client or the prospective client's representative that the information will not be treated as confidential information in the event the provider does not become a client and that providing such information will not preclude the licensee from being employed by a party adverse to the potential client in any current or future legal action or proceeding. For purposes of this section "reasonable notice" shall mean the following:

    (1) With respect to oral communications, including telephonic communications, reasonable notice consists of oral notice to the speaker given immediately by the licensee upon hearing that client information is being presented or will be presented.

    (2) With respect to written communications, including electronic and facsimile communications, reasonable notice consists of an oral or written notice to the sender within one business day.

(b) The licensee, on request, returns the original and all copies of documents provided by the prospective client or his or her representative within 30 days.

(c) The licensee does not utilize in any manner the information obtained, except that nothing shall prohibit the licensee from utilizing the same information obtained from an independent source such as through litigation discovery. (California Accountancy Act and Regulations §54)

Chart 7-9

DISCLOSURE OF CONFIDENTIAL INFORMATION

(a) No confidential information obtained by a licensee, in his or her professional capacity, concerning a client or a prospective client shall be disclosed by the licensee without the written permission of the client or prospective client, except for the following:

(1) disclosures made by a licensee in compliance with a subpoena or a summons enforceable by order of a court;

(2) disclosures made by a licensee regarding a client or prospective client to the extent that the licensee reasonably believes that it is necessary to maintain or defend himself/herself in a legal proceeding initiated by that client or prospective client;

(3) disclosures made by a licensee in response to an official inquiry from a federal or state government regulatory agency;

(4) disclosures made by a licensee or a licensee's duly authorized representative to another licensee in connection with a proposed sale or merger of the licensee's professional practice;

(5) disclosures made by a licensee to

(A) another licensee to the extent necessary for purposes of professional consultation and to

(B) professional standards review, ethics or quality control peer review organizations;

(6) disclosures made when specifically required by law;

(7) disclosures made at the direct request of the client to a person or entity that is designated by the client at the time of the request.

(b) In the event that confidential client information may be disclosed to persons or entities outside the United States in connection with the services provided, the licensee shall so inform the client in writing and obtain the client's written permission for the disclosure. (California Accountancy Act and Regulations §54.1)

What Would You Do 7-4 looks at a previous example while applying the California rules.

WHAT WOULD YOU DO 7-4

On the Train (Part 2)

Go back to What Would You Do 5-19. Did that CPA violate any California license rules? If so, how would anybody know? Did it do any harm?

How do you know what your workpapers are and what the client records are? What can you keep and what must you give back? Charts 7-10 and 7-11 discuss the California rules.

Chart 7-10

RECORD RETENTION

(a)   All statements, records, schedules, working papers and memoranda made by a licensee or a partner, shareholder, officer, director, or employee of a licensee, incident to, or in the course of, rendering services to a client in the practice of public accountancy, except the reports submitted by the licensee to the client and except for records which are part of the client's records, shall be and remain the property of the licensee in the absence of an express agreement between the licensee and the client to the contrary. No such statement, record, schedule, working paper, or memoranda shall be sold, transferred, or bequeathed, without the consent of the client or his or her personal representative or assignee, to anyone other than one or more surviving partners or stockholders or new partners or stockholders of the licensee, or any combined or merged firm or successor in interest to the licensee.

(b)   A licensee shall furnish to his or her client or former client, upon request and reasonable notice:

(1)   A copy of the licensee's working papers, to the extent that those working papers include records that would ordinarily constitute part of the client's records and are not otherwise available to the client.

(2) Any accounting or other records belonging to, or obtained from or on behalf of, the client which the licensee removed from the client's premises or received for the client's account. The licensee may make and retain copies of documents of the client when they form the basis for work done by him or her. (California Accountancy Act and Regulations §5037)

Chart 7-11

WORKING PAPERS

A licensee, after demand by or on behalf of a client, for books, records or other data, whether in written or machine sensible form, that are the client's records shall not retain such records. Unpaid fees do not constitute justification for retention of client records. Although, in general the accountant's working papers are the property of the licensee, if such working papers include records which would ordinarily constitute part of the client's books and records and are not otherwise available to the client, then the information on those working papers must be treated the same as if it were part of the client's books and records. (California Accountancy Act and Regulations §68)

What Would You Do 7-5 looks at how to handle a situation with a former client.

WHAT WOULD YOU DO 7-5

Client Information

You have provided your client, a restaurant, with bookkeeping and tax services over the past fifteen years. Suddenly you receive a letter from another CPA indicating that this client will no longer be using your services and requesting copies of all of your workpapers for the past three years. Your client still owes you for the tax returns you prepared last month. Needless to say, you are not pleased.

As you look at your workpapers, they consist of a tax program with your notes, copies of the client's bank reconciliations, their trial balance and financial statements. You also have adjusting journal entries, which were given to the client, and depreciation schedules, which were attached to the tax returns.

How would you respond to the letter? Which of these items do you feel you should provide to the new CPA? Describe why you feel that they should be provided.

Discussion Questions

1. If the accounting profession self-polices and has its own rules, why do states such as California need their own rules as well?

2. Describe the various designations an accountant in public practice can use. Which do you feel is best and why?

3. Name three ways an accountant can earn a commission and not violate California law.

4. Discuss what types of information must be reported to the board of accountancy. Why do you think this is an important requirement?

5. Describe three circumstances when a CPA must obtain a peer review. When is a peer review not required?

6. Is it possible to have a non-licensee as a member of an accounting firm? If so, how does that work?

7. In your opinion, what is adequate audit documentation?

8. According to California law, when is an accountant allowed to disclose confidential information? How does this differ from the AICPA standards?

9. At the end of tax season, you and your friends go out to celebrate. Unfortunately, you enjoy the evening a bit too much and, on the way home, are pulled over by the police. After given a sobriety test, you are arrested for felony DUI. Do you report this incident to the board of accountancy?

10. One morning a police officer and an attorney come by your office to discuss a client who owns a restaurant. They have evidence that the buyer is stealing from your client and want to talk about the internal control environment. You call your client, who says it is fine to discuss these matters. After a brief discussion of the internal control they ask for copies of cancelled checks so they can compare signatures. They also ask for copies of your client's personal and corporate tax returns.

    How would you respond to:

    a. discussing the internal control environment with them?
    b. providing copies of cancelled checks?
    c. giving them copies of the tax returns?

11. You are auditing an entity and looking at payroll transactions. You do not notice that, out of five employees, two have the same address. Your audit workpapers state that the checks are made out to the correct person and the proper amount. After the audit you discover that the two of them are related.

    Do you believe that your workpapers are adequate under the California Board of Accountancy rules? Why or why not?

Case Study[7]

Richard J. Rathman and the firm of Bernstein & Rathman, An Accountancy Corporation, were subject to disciplinary action for the willful failure to comply with professional standards, the Accountancy Act, and California Board of Accountancy Regulations by:

---

7. California Board of Accountancy Accusation AC-2016-38, December 28, 2017

a. repeated acts of negligence in their performance of an audit of a 401(k) profit-sharing plan for years ending December 31, 2011, and 2010;

b. departing from professional standards because they did not perform the audit in accordance with GAAS;

c. audit documentation that did not contain sufficient documentation to enable a reviewer with the relevant knowledge and experience, having no previous connection with the audit engagement, to understand the nature, timing extent and results of procedures performed, evidence obtained, and conclusions reached, and to determine the identity of the persons who performed and reviewed the work;

d. reporting on a Peer Review Reporting form dated September 25, 2014, that the highest level of accounting and auditing services provided in the previous three years was a compilation with disclosures when they had issued the September 6, 2012, auditor's report for the Department of Labor; and

e. obtaining an Engagement Peer Review when they should have obtained a System Peer Review.

They were put on probation with the following terms:

a. After 3 years' probation, both Rathman and his corporation are prohibited from performing audits, reviews, or other attestation services unless they petition for reinstatement.

b. Complete and provide proper documentation of twenty-four hours of continuing education in the subject matter of compilations.

c. Complete four hours of continuing education in ethics.

d. Complete an approved Regulatory Review course.

e. Be subject to peer review by a Board-recognized peer review program.

f. Reimburse the California Board of Accountancy $7,093 for its investigation and prosecution costs.

Case Study Questions

1. What sections of the California Accountancy Act and Regulations did the firm violate?

2. How would you advise them to ensure that they comply with the rules in the future?

CHAPTER 8

ETHICAL LEADERSHIP
AND ACCOUNTING

Good actions give strength to ourselves and inspire good actions in others.
—Plato, Greek philosopher (428–328 BC)

So far, we have discussed theories and rules related to ethics. This chapter puts together the concepts and applies them specifically to leadership and the accounting profession.

What Is Ethical Leadership?

Part of being an accounting professional is problem-solving, and ethical problem-solving is always a part of that process. Being an ethical leader means building an environment where those in the organization feel comfortable talking to others, not just for technical advice but also to discuss ethical solutions to problems. Accountants and auditors generally have pretty high ethical values, but these values mean nothing unless there is a supportive organization to assist in putting those values into action.

When conflicts exist, voicing your opinion will create challenges that can be aggravated by an indifferent boss or an organizational culture that operates by rationalizing unethical actions. Pressures imposed by management under the guise of "It is expected practice around here" or "You need to be a team player" can challenge your values.

Building trust is a critical component of an ethical manager. With consistency, credibility, and predictability in relationships, everybody, from the top down, should feel comfortable expressing their opinions. In addition, openness, respect, and fair treatment of others will help create an environment where actions and decisions can be questioned without fear of reprisal.

Ethical leaders attempt to do the right thing and communicate to others that the right thing is going to happen all the time. The "right reason" is not to maximize profits or increase stock price but, instead, to build a culture that creates the kind of environment that supports ethical decision-making.

By being visible to employees, an ethical leader will be a role model for ethical conduct. They should communicate regularly, and persuasively, with employees about ethical standards, principles, and values. That leader should use reward systems to hold employees accountable. A code of conduct may be in place, but an ethical leader will also understand that doing the right thing requires action.

A distinguishing characteristic of many of the accounting cases in this book is that short-term factors were allowed to compromise long-term ethical values. CPAs and others acted based on non-ethical values, such as enhancing share prices and creating personal wealth. Employees "held their nose" and carried out unethical orders that led to fraud, managed earnings and illegal actions. Leaders at places like Enron, WorldCom and Tyco created an environment that sent the message "all is well" while the company was collapsing around them.

Building a reputation for ethical leadership means enabling ethics and values to exist while competing fairly and meeting financial projections. During many of the accounting scandals, the goal was to meet or beat analysts' earnings expectations. All kinds of financial shenanigans were used to accomplish that goal; some companies even turned to non-GAAP measures of earnings, such as EBITDA[1], to project the image of exceeding expectations. And many companies continue to do so today.

Ethical leaders are individuals who are:

---

1. Earnings Before Interest, Depreciation and Amortization

1. aware of how they think and behave;
2. perceived by others as being aware of their own and others' values/moral perspectives, knowledge and strengths;
3. aware of the context in which they operate;
4. confident, optimistic, resilient and, at times, courageous;
5. able to take seriously their responsibilities;
6. able to recognize and evaluate ethical issues; and
7. willing to take moral actions that are based on their beliefs and values.

Ethical leaders are concerned with achieving a common good for the group for which they are responsible and/or the entire organization. This leadership results in positive ethical effects in followers, which, in turn, influence the ethical organization environment. Followers are likely to emulate the example of leaders who set a high ethical standard and make ethical choices on their own without the input of the leader.

Trust is a key component in developing successful relationships between leaders and followers. A trusting relationship is built on shared values, respect, open communication, and accountability.

The perception of a leader's legitimacy might play an important role in determining how the leader's actions are interpreted and the influence they have on followers. For example, imagine if a controller was pressured by the CPA who paid no regard to ethical standards. When they see this, the followers would be less likely to embrace, much less respect, the actions of the leader.

Case 8-1

ENRON[2]

Enron exhibited unusual corporate ethics. They had a policy nicknamed "rank and yank", where employees gave each other annual ratings; based on these ratings, the bottom 15% were fired. Every year, all employees were rated from 1 (best) to 5 (worst). The more money you made for the company, the better your rating. Jeff Skilling, the president and CEO, was fond of saying that money was the only thing that motivated people; he mandated that between 10 and 15% of the employees had to be rated as 5's. And to get a rating of 5 meant that you were fired.

---

2. John Powers, "Rank and Yank at Enron," *LA Weekly, January 9, 2002, http://www.laweekly. com/news/rank-and-yank-at-enron-2134275.*

Ethical Leadership in Accounting

In public accounting, rules and processes have been developed with the sole aim of limiting audit risk and guaranteeing audit quality. Responsible leadership in accounting and audit firms means going beyond the rules and creating an ethical environment. For example, encouraging employees to ask probing questions when management's representations are unclear or unsubstantiated is important for not only a quality work product but also making ethical choices.

Research has found that audit seniors' perceptions of their firm leaders and firm culture impact their behavior. But what happens when individual values do not fit into the expectations of the firm? As seen in Chart 8-1, this could lead the individual to alter their behavior to conform to the accounting firm's norms; the alternative, most likely, would be to be fired or quit.

Chart 8-1

SENIOR AUDITORS[3]

One hundred twenty practicing senior auditors representing the Big Four firms, other international firms, large regional firms, and local firms were asked to indicate the frequency of selected unethical behavior among audit seniors.

The results showed that a typical audit senior at these firms more frequently underreports time than signing off on audit work that was not properly performed. The more they felt their firms were ethical, the less unethical audit behavior they felt compelled to undertake.

Internal auditors can sometimes be bullied or coerced by CFOs, which makes it more difficult for them to follow their own ethics. Case 8-2 is an illustration of how this worked and when one CPA had the courage to fight back.

---

3. Jan Taylor Morris, "The Impact of Authentic Leadership and Ethical Firm Culture on Auditor Behavior," *Journal of Behavioral Studies in Business 7 (September 2014): 1–32.*

Case 8-2

WORLDCOM

Cynthia Cooper was the head of internal audit at WorldCom. She was consistently pressured by her boss to not act on improper accounting findings by her team. An internal auditor with a weak character might go along, but Cooper demonstrated strong ethical leadership skills by working with her team to uncover the scope of the fraud. She wouldn't take no for an answer and went to the audit committee first, then to the outside auditors, and persisted in her efforts to correct and expose the wrongdoing.

When deciding whether to record a questionable journal entry (i.e., any entry for which a reasonable business case can be made for either recording it or not recording it), accountants and auditors may take their cue from management's behavior, especially if such behavior is the norm and has been rewarded in the past. For instance, accountants may hesitate to record a questionable entry if they know that an internal audit is likely to detect inappropriate financial reporting practices.

Case 8-3

HEALTHSOUTH[4]

Former chief internal auditor Teresa Rubio Sanders, who was hired in 1990 and quit in late 1999, testified that her office wasn't allowed to see the general ledger, where there was a $2.7 billion earnings overstatement from 1996 through 2002. Internal auditors working under her were assigned to check bathrooms and parking lots for trash but lacked access to corporate books where the fraud occurred.

Sanders testified she never complained to HealthSouth directors about the lack of access to corporate records. She also said she rarely met with directors or the audit committee.

---

4. Jay Reeves, "Ex-HealthSouth Exec Details Fraud," *The Seattle Times, February 24, 2005, https://www.seattletimes.com/business/ex-healthsouth-exec-details-fraud/.*

Notice how Sanders lack of concern shows the importance of ethical leadership in the internal audit function. CPAs like Sanders, who bury their head in the sand while fraud occurs, not only fail in their ethical leadership role but also make it more difficult for the external auditors to uncover what is still hidden under the surface.

Even in tax practice there is disconnect between the perceptions of organizational ethics among the higher and lower levels of an organization. As seen in Chart 8-2, employees at higher levels perceive a higher level of organizational ethics.

Chart 8-2

TAX ACCOUNTING[5]

A study found that, when describing an ethical dilemma, there is disconnect between tax partners and staff about their perceptions of organizational ethics. On average, tax partners rated the ethical environments of their firms as stronger than staff tax practitioners, especially with respect to firm leadership. Those who did describe an ethical dilemma rated the ethical environment as weaker.

In a follow-up study it was found that, when staff believe they have a meaningful role in shaping and maintaining the ethical environment of their firms and/or have a strong organizational fit with the firm, they are more likely to perceive the ethical environment as strong. The study also found that, among firm leaders (i.e., tax partners), the sense of having a stronger public interest responsibility and a higher frequency of receiving mentoring are both associated with stronger perceptions of the ethical environment.

Summing It up

Ethical organizations encourage employees to voice their values. Ethical leaders know that if employees feel comfortable speaking up about matters of concern in a supportive environment, problems will not fester and the likelihood of unethical activity is lessened.

---

5. Donna D. Bobek and Robin R. Radtke, "An Experiential Investigation of the Ethical Environment of Tax Professionals," *Journal of American Tax Association 29, no. 2 (Fall 2007):* *63–84.*

Because of the distance between the parties, a manager who feels that he or she is a moral person is not enough to encourage the ethical behavior of followers. Managers gain legitimacy only if employees believe they are principled, caring, say what they will do and do what they say. They not only "talk the talk" but also "walk the walk."

Consistency in words and actions underlies ethical leadership. Followers must be comfortable that, if they follow the ethical path, they will be rewarded for doing so. In most of the cases discussed in this book, the opposite was true

When people face a moral problem, they sometimes have a tough time not confusing moral goals, values, feelings, and emotions with problem-solving and decision-making. This happens frequently and conflicting pressures make the situation more difficult. However, these skills can be learned. They require practice, commitment, reflection, and continuous re-examination as to whether you need to adjust your thinking to match the ethical demands you feel comfortable with.

Let your behavior match your values and beliefs.

Discussion Questions

1. Choose a company you believe is ethical, and give specific examples why you think so.

2. Why might a manager fail to establish an ethical culture in an organization?

3. Name three reasons why there might be an ethical leadership failure in a company and how these might be prevented.

4. Describe the role of professional judgment in accounting ethics.

5. How does the nature of the internal audit function influence whether an auditor will record undocumented journal entries?

6. How might the culture of an accounting firm influence a tax accountant's judgment?

7. What do you think is the most important factor in a firm's culture? Why?

8. How might ethical traits of different leaders influence the type of earnings management the company engages in?

9. Describe, in ethical terms, the sort of accounting firm you would like to work for.

10. What ethical dilemmas have you faced this week? How did you handle them? Would you have done anything differently?

11. A brand new client takes salary advances from his professional corporation, showing them as loans throughout the year. In December of every year, he shows the amount as salary and pays the taxes. As the new CPA you are aware that this is fairly common, but, if audited, the IRS would probably assess penalties.

    What ethical issues does this present? Does the precedent of the prior CPA factor into your decision as to how you would handle this situation?

12. You are the controller of a nonprofit organization. Every month the actual results are compared to the monthly budget and the annual budget. A new executive director is hired who changes the monthly budgets after receiving the actual number from you; in other words, the two match every month.

    How might the ethical values of the organization be reconciled with this action? What options are available to you?

13. As the outside CPA of a medical practice, you cannot help but notice cash receipts drop off to virtually nothing every December and then the first week of January cash collections are huge. You ask the office manager, who says that the doctor insists that any checks received after Thanksgiving be held until the first week of January, thus deferring the income to the following year. They justify the action by saying the cash gets into the bank, and the only real issue is the year it is shown as income.

    What do you think about the ethical values of this organization? If you were a patient and knew this information, how might that change your feelings about the doctor? As the accountant, how should you approach this?

Case Study

The top two former officers of CUC International Inc. were accused of directing a massive financial fraud while selling millions of dollars' worth of the company's common stock. For the period 1995–1997 alone, pre-tax operating income reported to the public by CUC was inflated by an aggregate amount of over $500 million.[6]

CUC merged with HFS Incorporated on December 17, 1997, to form Cendant Corporation. Upon disclosure of the fraud, the price of Cendant common stock plummeted, causing billions of dollars in losses for investors.

CUC's chairman and chief executive officer directed the fraud from its beginnings in 1985. From at least 1991 on, CUC's president and chief operating officer, joined the chairman in directing the scheme. The following are some of the ways it was done:

1. Personally reviewing and managing schedules listing fraudulent adjustments to be made to CUC's quarterly and annual financial statements. CUC senior management used the adjustments to artificially pump up income and earnings, defrauding investors by creating the illusion of a company that had ever-increasing earnings and making millions for themselves along the way.

2. Undertaking a program of mergers and acquisitions on behalf of CUC in order to generate inflated merger and purchase reserves at CUC. Forbes and Shelton sought out one merger partner (HFS) because they believed the reserves that would be created would be big enough to bury the fraud. To entice the HFS management into the merger, they artificially increased CUC's current year earnings as well as future earnings projections. Soon after the merger, they explicitly congratulated each other on being masterful "financial engineers" who had been able to nurture the fraud through the years and who had assured their continued success by duping HFS into agreeing to a merger with CUC.

3. Profiting from their own wrongdoing. They sold CUC and Cendant securities at inflated prices while the fraud they directed was underway and

---

6. Securities and Exchange Commission Litigation Release No. 16910, *Securities and Exchange Commission v. Walter A. Forbes and E. Kirk Shelton, Accounting and Auditing Enforcement Release No. 1372 Civil Action No. 01-987, February 28, 2001.*

undisclosed. These sales brought executives millions of dollars in ill-gotten gains.

The SEC found that Cendant violated many provisions of federal securities laws. In addition to the final judgment against the officers, a class action suit was settled for $2.85 billion, the largest case ever to that date. In addition, the auditor, Ernst & Young, paid Cendant almost $300 million.

Case Study Questions

1. Do you believe that income smoothing an ethical practice? Are there times when it might be considered ethical and others when it might not be?

2. Income smoothing is just shifting income from one year to another. What is wrong with that?

3. Analyze the management actions from the perspective of these Fraud Triangle discussed in Chapter 3.

4. Even though they paid a fine, do you think the auditors met their ethical obligations? Why or why not?

CASES

INDEX

ABOUT THE AUTHOR

 In 1979, Howard J. Levine formed an accounting firm in the Los Angeles area. Until its sale in 2016, the office was well known for bookkeeping, accounting, tax return preparation, tax planning and consulting for small businesses, partnerships and corporations, as well as tax exempt (non-profit) organizations and private foundations.

As a college professor and in private practice, plus with experience with national accounting firms, Howard created a diverse client base and a wealth of experience, providing accounting and tax services to a unique group of clients nationwide. These clients ranged from small retail businesses, physicians, restaurants and a variety of service businesses, to non-profit organizations and private foundations with budgets from under $100,000 to assets over $100 million.

Howard has served as both a member and Southern California coordinator of the Technical Review Panel of the California Board of Accountancy. He has written questions used on the CPA examination and has served on the board of numerous organizations as board member, treasurer and president. Howard served as a trustee of the California Society of CPAs Group Insurance Trust and as a member of the Internal Revenue Service Taxpayer Advocacy Panel.

Howard is currently a professor of accounting at Los Angeles Valley College. He is a CPA as well as a diplomat and life member of the American Board of Forensic Accountants.

Made in the USA
Las Vegas, NV
14 January 2024

84333727R00116